ARE YOU
MAKE A M

❯❯❯❯❯❯❯❯❯❯❯❯❯❯❯❯❯❯❯❯❯❯❯❯❯❯❯❯❯

Are you considering a job or career change?

Have you been offered a promotion within your department or to another division within your company?

Are you a college-age individual about to start out on your career?

Are you considering reentering the workforce?

Are you a working parent who needs to find a job and company compatible with your family and child-care obligations?

Have you outgrown your present job? Are you in the market for new challenges, greater responsibilities, richer rewards?

IF YOU'RE READY TO FIND THE PERFECT JOB, YOU'RE READY FOR
THE RIGHT MOVE.

Also by Michael Zey:

THE MENTOR CONNECTION

THE RIGHT MOVE

MOVE

How to Find the Perfect Job

Michael G. Zey, Ph.D.

IVY BOOKS • NEW YORK

Ivy Books
Published by Ballantine Books
Copyright © 1987 by Michael G. Zey

Library of Congress Catalog Card Number: 86-29015

ISBN-0-8041-0224-4

This edition published by arrangement with Franklin Watts, Inc.

Manufactured in the United States of America

First Ballantine Books Edition: April 1988

CONTENTS

◆◆◆◆◆◆◆◆◆◆◆◆◆◆◆◆◆◆◆◆◆◆◆◆◆◆◆◆◆

PREFACE   vii

CHAPTER 1
Making the Right Move   1

CHAPTER 2
To Leave or Not to Leave   10

CHAPTER 3
In Search of the Excellent Company   41

CHAPTER 4
Getting Your Just Rewards   64

CHAPTER 5
Make Sure You Can Do the Job   97

CHAPTER 6
What You Must Know About Company Politics   126

CHAPTER 7
The Job and Your Life   145

CHAPTER 8
A Satisfying Job   175

CHAPTER 9
A Question of Style   191

CHAPTER 10
The Job as a Stepping-stone   222

CHAPTER 11
Putting It All Together   238

CHAPTER 12
When Staying in Your Current Job Is the Right Move   266

INDEX   281

PREFACE

◆◆◆◆◆◆◆◆◆◆◆◆◆◆◆◆◆◆◆◆◆◆◆◆◆

I was inspired to write this book by the job-hunting experiences of the countless individuals I encountered over the years—executives, managers, students, and new entrants into the job market—who seemed to be having problems finding the job and company that would make them happy. Their job searches were usually "guided" by questionable advice from head-hunters, friends, interviewers, and family members and often resulted in what turned out to be career mistakes.

Oddly enough, some of the worst career advice came not from people but from books. Many of the books were essentially lists of good or "excellent" companies that the job hunter was advised to assault with letters, résumés, and phone calls. After reviewing several of these "best of" books—the best company for female managers, the best company for entrepreneurs, the companies with the fastest track for promotion—I realized that they all had shortcomings in their ability to help the job hunter find the appropriate position.

Their limits are many. First of all, if the company you are considering is not on a "best of" list, you are no better off making a decision than if you had never reviewed the book. Second, even if you *are* considering a company mentioned in such a book, you really cannot use these broad descriptions to learn about the politics, culture, and style of the department or division you will be working for. Third, these books often overlook one or more crucial dimensions that you should be considering in choosing a corporation. And last, most of these books give you scarcely a hint about how to plan your career systematically.

This book overcomes these drawbacks by taking a completely different approach. Instead of looking only at specific companies, it examines company characteristics that are crucial to your decision to take a job. It will show you how the interviewers, the press, your personal networks, and other sources can provide valuable information about the pay, perks, politics, corporate culture, and financial status of any prospective employer. It will also help you gain insight into what you want in regard to all these work dimensions.

The book is based on solid research. I interviewed employees in real companies along with dozens of personnel directors, headhunters, and job seekers. I also made liberal use of the popular and business press. .

WHO SHOULD READ THIS BOOK

This book is aimed at managers, workers, professionals, and others who want to make the right move. You may have three job offers in hand or may have just begun your job search. Whatever stage you are at in the job-hunting process, you can use this book to make the right career decision.

Specifically, this book can help you if you are in any of the following situations:

1. You are considering a job or career change
2. You have just been offered a promotion within your department or to another division within your company
3. You are a college-age individual about to start your career and are unsure of how to evaluate the job offers you are receiving
4. You are someone who is considering reentering the workforce and wants to make a good new career decision
5. You are a working parent who needs to find a job and company compatible with your family and child care obligations
6. You are any of the countless people who have outgrown their jobs and wish to make sure your next job is the right move

WHAT THIS BOOK WILL HELP YOU DO

If you heed the lessons presented in this volume, it should prove valuable to you in several ways. It will help you evaluate your current job and decide whether you should consider looking elsewhere. In addition, the advice in this book should help you evaluate new offers and continually reassess any jobs, including the ones you choose with its guidance. And, most important, with the help of this book, you will learn about yourself, your abilities, your needs, and your goals. After all, only when you know what you really want can you ever hope to make the right move.

THE RIGHT MOVE

How to Find the Perfect Job

CHAPTER I

◆◆◆◆◆◆◆◆◆◆◆◆◆◆◆◆◆◆◆◆◆◆◆◆◆◆

Making the Right Move

We put a great deal of thought into the decisions we make in our lives. If we decide to get married, we experience profound anxiety about the type of man or woman who will be our mate. We carefully consider everything, including the person's looks, values, goals, and family background. We worry whether the person is as attracted to us as we are to them—and if we are attracted for the "right" reasons.

When buying a car, most of us invest extensive time in perusing *Consumer Reports* to compare vehicles on the basis of average repair rates, miles per gallon, satisfaction levels of current owners, and style. Once we have made a tentative choice, we go from showroom to showroom bargaining and comparing prices, options, and warranties.

Sometimes a friend or acquaintance will inform us that they bought a car on the spur of the moment, without checking reliability reports or doing comparison shopping. We hope that our friend made the right choice but sense in our heart of hearts that only with luck will the purchase be a satisfactory one.

The average person approaches the purchase of a house with the same careful deliberation he or she applies to other major life decisions. Many of us spend months looking at homes, studying neighborhoods, investigating mortgages, and making certain that the school system is good for the kids. None of us would make a decision based on price alone, ignoring such issues as the quality of the neighborhood or the length of the commute from this new home to our jobs.

One would think that people would take as much time and care when selecting their jobs and employers. After all, work has become an increasingly important part of all our lives. More people are in the work force than ever before. Even women with young children not yet in school are more likely than not to be working. The full-time homemaker is disappearing, along with the early retiree, the endowed widow, and the nonworking student. Work has achieved a new level of importance for everybody.

But many of us give much less thought to selecting a job than we do to picking a house or car. Many of the individuals I have researched have encountered unforeseen problems in their jobs merely because they did not apply the same care to their job choice as they did to other major life decisions.

Take the example of a young business professional who—after working several years as a director of marketing with an academic publishing firm—was offered a marketing position with a midsize publishing house. The publisher claimed that it wanted to become more trade- and general-audience-oriented and thought he was just the person to take charge of this transformation. He accepted the job but, to his surprise, for the next few years met frustration at every turn. He was hampered by lack of staff and a low budget and, worse, by the company's vacillating commitment to the goals it had seemingly endorsed when he was first hired. After two years the company let the young manager go, giving him no more explanation for his dismissal than that his appointment "did not work out the way we had hoped."

Could he have avoided what turned out to be a career disaster? I think so. If you look closely at his story, you will notice that it was the company's lack of direction that eventually brought down his career. If he had kept his eyes and ears open to the subtle hints of a poor corporate culture and weak political environment revealed during the interview process, he could have saved himself a great deal of grief.

Corporate politics is not the only criterion you must consider to make the right move. Many times you will accept or reject a position based on whether it fits in with the rest of your life. It is not uncommon for an otherwise excellent offer to clash with some of your other life priorities. One of my respondents, a director of employee relations at a pharmaceutical corporation, was offered a tantalizing position as vice president of human resources for a multinational electronics corporation, at a salary nearly double her current pay. But to earn this $100,000, she would have had to move from the New York metropolitan area to what she considered the "boonies." And, while undergoing her series of interviews, she learned that the company, which relied heavily on government defense contracts, was being investigated by the Justice Department for price-fixing and contract fraud.

This person was obviously in a quandary about how to make the right move. Though her current salary was adequate, she found this new offer extremely tempting. However, she suddenly realized that other values, especially those related to her life-style, were beginning to assume an importance equal to that of her annual salary. She eventually turned down the offer. We will be dealing throughout with how to make similar types of life decisions that pit financial concerns against such priorities as family, relationships, and personal comfort.

Even people just starting their careers, often right out of high school and college, are confronted with critical career decisions. I interviewed one such young woman who was offered an entry-level media analyst position at a prestigious television rating company. The starting salary was average, but the opportunity for advancement and salary increases seemed good. She was about to take the job when she was offered a market research position with a three-year-old telemarketing company that had undergone exponential growth in this volatile industry.

Her priorities were not very complicated. She wanted to find the best-paying job, in her chosen field, with a company that promised personal career growth. But even with these well-defined goals, she still had to gather much information about the companies, their career ladders, and their promotional policies to finally make a sound decision.

Like these three people, millions of other workers, managers, homemakers, and recent college graduates are confronted with one of the most crucial decisions in their lives: What job and company should they choose that will afford them the best chance of career success? What factors are the most important in making this decision? In short, how do they know they are making the right move?

You Can Learn the Skill of Making the Right Move

Whether you are a young worker just entering the work force or a seasoned veteran looking to make a big career change, you can increase the chances that the next job and company you choose constitute the right move.

Making an informed choice depends on your ability to ask the right questions about a company—and on getting correct answers. And if you are currently employed, making the right move also depends on deciding whether the positions you are considering surpass your present job on the dimensions that you think important.

By the time you have finished reading this book and digesting the material presented in it, you will be sensitized to those factors you should consider when selecting a position and company. Equally important, if you are currently employed, by book's end you will be more certain about whether you should leave your current job. Occasionally, the right move is no move at all.

We will focus on those factors crucial to your happiness and satisfaction with the prospective position, such as pay, promotion, perks, and politics. In addition, some chapters will help you determine whether your prospective company's corporate culture and style are compatible with your own values and work habits.

You must ask many questions about the job and company to be certain that you are making the right choice. What will it be like to perform this job, at this company, for the next few years? And is the company about to expand or about to fold?

Throughout, we will look at the strategies and tactics involved in gathering information about prospective jobs and companies. How do you get a financial report on a company? How do you find out about a company's day-care facilities? And how do you know if your prospective position will open the doors of career success at the company?

Changing Times Demand New Strategies

It's tough making job choices today. Because the economy and society of the 1980s are in a state of flux, you the job hunter require a fresh approach to your career. Just look at some of the major trends and you will realize why you need to adopt new strategies to make the right move.

The first major trend is the changing composition of the work force. You may be among the growing group of students, women, and others just entering the work force who genuinely need a method to evaluate job offers. So many recent studies are unable to explain why men on average are doing better than women in income and job rank. One of the possible answers is that women and other new entrants into the job market just don't have the skills and knowledge to make the best choice when considering a job. They do not have the networks that could direct them to the best company or job. Many of these new entrants are not even aware of what dimensions they ought to be considering when choosing a job.

Also undergoing a fundamental transformation are the very natures of jobs and companies. You may next find yourself working in one of the increasing number of new companies that have excellent growth potential but are too small or too new for you to get extensive information on them. Certainly you wouldn't find this type of company on any "best of" list.

However, there are ways to know whether taking a job with a brand-new company with high growth potential is the right move. You will find out how in Chapter 3, "In Search of the Excellent Company."

Changing social and economic conditions are also tranforming the priorities with which you will have to be concerned when picking your next job. Like many other workers, you will be increasingly concerned with a variety of nonpay aspects of the job. For example, over half the executives polled over the last year or two have refused job relocation, even when such geographic shifts would have brought them substantial increases in pay and position. They were taking into consideration a number of new priorities, including their spouses' careers, the quality of life they were currently enjoying, and the effect of a move on family stability.

You will probably want to consider many of these same issues when choosing a job. This book will highlight many nonpay issues—such as a company's relocation policy, day-care allowances, culture, and political climate, to name but a few—that you should research before making a career move. It will also examine some of the many methods of performing such research.

Your Job Hunt Is a Lifetime Activity

Can we ever hope to find the "perfect job," one that meets all our expectations and fulfills all our requirements? I would respond that although you can find a job that is ideal for you at the time you take it several factors conspire to make any job only temporarily perfect at best. As you will see, your job search is a lifelong activity.

What makes a job perfect at one time and undesirable at another is simply change—in yourself, in the position, and in the job market. Take your own requirements as an example. A job could be perfect for you at this time of your life. But you may someday become totally dissatisfied with the selfsame job for no other reason than that you and your needs have changed. You may not consider a high salary as important as you once did, you may no longer want independence on the job, or the large office and other status symbols may have lost their luster.

You may also have become more skilled and experienced since you first took the job. If this is so, your increased marketability may make you hungry to leave and move ahead to bigger and better things. You have simply outgrown the job. And an improved job market, one that provides viable alternatives to your current situation, can dampen your original enthusiasm about your company and job.

The organization itself may change over time. Mergers, personnel changes, and new policies can make the company much less inviting than when you originally signed on. Your employer's pay structure, promotional practices, corporate culture, and political climate may all have changed for the worse since you first took the job. You may also have discovered faults in the company that you didn't know existed when you first came on board.

So there really isn't a perfect job, only one that meets your needs at a particular stage of your life. No job is a terminal point. Even when you land the job that meets all your needs, you must still continue to evaluate it.

This book is written so that you can use it throughout your career to perform such personal and organizational assessments. Refer to this volume over the years as a trusty guide to your job and career. As the job market changes, as your new position becomes transformed, and—more important—as you change and your work and personal values develop, you will have this book to help you make the right move.

CHAPTER 2

▶▶▶▶▶▶▶▶▶▶▶▶▶▶▶▶▶▶▶▶▶▶▶▶

To Leave or Not to Leave

How many people do you know who dislike their jobs? Probably a significant number. They complain, they threaten to leave, and they become increasingly miserable. But they stay in their jobs, because they can't find another position, hope things will get better, and are afraid to move.

Invariably, they become disgruntled with their jobs and begin calling in sick regularly, coming to work late, and acting miserable with their coworkers. Their work, self-esteem, and even their health suffers. Some even quit out of frustration, regardless of whether they have another position lined up.

THE PUSH-PULL FACTOR

But most of us wait until something better comes along. We cannot even leave an unbearable work situation without an alternative, because we all have familial, financial, and other obligations that force us to continue working. For most of us, unemployment is not a viable option.

Others of us are not unhappy at work but are still waiting for something good to happen to us, either at our present jobs or in the future with another company. Many of us are neither terribly happy nor unhappy, just waiting to see if things will improve.

You may fall into one of the above categories. If you are considering leaving your job, you will constantly be weighing two different issues: the quality of the job you now have and the relative attractiveness of the offers you are receiving or are entertaining.

I call this the push-pull factor of job hunting: The decision to take a job is based on the quality of your present job in relation to the desirability of your other job opportunities. In other words, you may want to leave because you are being "pushed" by the undesirability of your current job or "pulled" by the attractiveness of another offer.

In fact, throughout your career you are pushed and pulled by any number of factors. For instance, you may have no real opportunities to leave your job at the current time but know deep down that your current position is less than perfect or perhaps even intolerable. This is a push factor.

Or your current position may be everything you ever wanted in a job or company until you either read a newspaper ad describing a new position, get a call from a headhunter, or find out that a friend's company is offering a better career opportunity or more money than your current situation. To the extent that you are considering leaving your job because of the attractiveness of another position, we can speak of the pull aspects of career change.

The right move deals with these two broad aspects of the job hunt. This chapter deals with the push aspect—those factors in your current situation that may suggest that it is time to move on. The rest of the book will help you evaluate the pull factors—those jobs and companies that are tempting you to leave your company.

You should be concerned about a number of factors when making the decision to leave or stay with your company. When evaluating their situation, most people first consider the company's economic health and their own career track. These two elements are usually the areas in which job dissatisfaction first surfaces.

How Successful Is Your Company?

People jump off sinking ships, run out of burning buildings, parachute out of crashing airplanes, and evacuate their towns during flood warnings. The aforementioned situations are usually obvious to people who keep their eyes and ears open. Such disasters present themselves quite plainly. Yet, working for a company that is stagnating or heading for disaster poses another type of danger, not necessarily to life and limb but certainly to our financial security and our chances for success.

The first question you must ask when deciding to make a career move is whether the company is growing, stagnating, or headed for pure disaster.

A variety of conditions may be a cause of worry. The company may be on the verge of bankruptcy, it may slowly be heading that way, or it may be entering a period of slow growth or out-and-out stagnation. In any event, these conditions can inhibit your career now or in the future. After all, a company that is either not growing or decreasing in size tends not to be the kind of place on which to pin your career hopes. But how do you determine whether your company is in trouble? And conversely, how can you tell whether your company has growth potential?

YOUR COMPANY'S FINANCIAL HEALTH

Your decision to stay with your company may very well be based on its general economic health. Its current and future profitability and its prospects for long-term growth should be critical factors in your decision to leave your company. Here are some questions you must ask about your company's finances when making the decision to leave or not to leave.

▶ Is the Company Now Showing a Profit?

This information should not be very difficult for you as an employee to get your hands on. Quarterly and annual reports to stockholders should help you gain an understanding of how well the company is doing financially.

In addition, heed well the rumors and gossip that form the basis of the corporate grapevine. In this regard, it wouldn't hurt you to have access to a friendly higher-up or two, insiders who can give you some information about the company's prospects.

You should approach this issue as if you were a regular corporate stockholder who has a large stake in the company's future. In point of fact, though you may not

be a stockholder you most certainly are a "stake-
holder." Your future is tied to the general health of
your company.

◗ Will It Show a Profit in the Near Future?

It is not as easy to gauge your company's future economic health as it is to assess its current fiscal standing.
But you must be able to ascertain the extent to which
you can bank your future on your company's long-term
prospects.

It is difficult to predict how well any economic enterprise will perform over a two- to three-year period.
The company could have hidden profits or hidden
losses. Short-term losses caused by company spending
on plant and equipment very often appear to the un-
trained eye to be an economic debacle, when in fact
the company is merely investing in the future.

In the next chapter we will deal with how to gauge
industry growth and market share specifically. You can
use these indicators to predict the success of your current company or any prospective employer.

◗ What Does the Popular Press Say About Your Company's Financial Health?

If you have exhausted the rumor mills and the stock
reports, you might want to consult the popular press to
settle any doubts you may have about your company's
financial future.

Very often the popular business press has information garnered by insiders within your company, people
who either knowingly or unwittingly pass corporate intelligence to the staff members of a newsletter, paper,
or magazine. Even if you finally decide that staying in
your organization is the right move, the information

you gather concerning your company's finances will make this effort well worth your time. Employees who gather this type of information are usually able to use it to identify the best projects to become involved with or the best product line to get transferred to. (For an annotated listing of popular and business press sources, refer to the next chapter.)

◆ Is There an Unfriendly Takeover in the Future?

Nothing could make your leaving the company more the right move than doing so immediately before an unfriendly takeover. If you are an executive, be aware that the majority of executives in overtaken companies either get fired at takeover or "resign" within the first twelve months.

Be aware of the signs of takeover: weakness in your division, inability to compete in the field, and news that a predatory conglomerate has been showing interest in your company. Often there are economic signs of impending takeover. If your company has a large amount of undervalued assets, it may be ripe for takeover.

The problem with takeovers is that often the absorbed company seems completely healthy. It's just that a healthier company buys it out. Again, rumors often precede the takeover; rarely does something like this happen overnight.

One aspect of takeovers that makes your career planning difficult is knowing who is taking over whom. The relationship between General Motors and EDP is a classic example. General Motors took over EDP, but not merely to add another company to its acquisition list. The general management of GM really wanted to integrate EDP's data-processing capabilities into its corporate operations. In the process, EDP managers were brought in over some GM managers to oversee the implementation of data-processing procedures into the GM organizational structure. So, although GM bought EDP, it was the GM managers who were threatened with job loss.

Most of the time the results of a takeover are less ambiguous. When a conglomerate like Allied absorbs a company, there is very little question whose employees will get laid off. And certain employees are more vulnerable than others. For instance, staff positions are usually the first to go. As one executive from a particularly predatory company told me, there is no need for two legal departments, two human resources departments, or two accounting departments. So the lawyers, personnel professionals, and accountants in the bought company are usually out on the street right after the merger.

If you are now in a situation in which your company has already been taken over, you should examine closely your position in the new company. The second part of this chapter, which presents questions regarding your organizational status, is particularly relevant if your company has just been absorbed by another.

◆ Does Your Company Regularly Sell Off Divisions?

If your corporation has a tendency to buy and sell divisions, be advised to keep your career options open. Very often the sold division is given a brand-new management team by the purchasing company. If you are a manager in the sold division, your career there could be in jeopardy.

If you are in a nonmanagement position, you may be more fortunate. The clerical and support staff and the lower echelons of the corporation are often left intact by the buying company. But if you are in middle management or above, keep your options open in both the takeover and the sold division situations.

YOUR COMPANY'S ABILITY TO EXPAND

When assessing your company's economic health, you should definitely be concerned about whether your company can expand both its product line and its market. Profit statements alone can be deceptive.

While this may not be a major problem if your company is aggressively marketing its products, some companies definitely need new products in order to be competitive. For instance, some companies produce "tried and true" products and do not have to expand their research-and-development staff to obtain positive grades on their economic prospects. But if you are working for a computer software company or an electronics firm, you will definitely want to know whether it is committed to expansion in size and product line.

▶ Is the Company Facing Difficult Economic Conditions?

Think about the overall economic environment facing your company. This environment, and your company's adaptability to it, are crucial to whether you leave or stay.

Does your company have the mechanisms to sense changes in the market? Does it regularly monitor the competition? Do other companies always seem just one step ahead? Many companies—the successful ones—have strong market research departments to help them analyze and monitor changes in the economic environment and in the public's tastes.

◗ Do You Think Your Company Has the Will to Change?

If your company is facing tough economic conditions, tighter government regulations, stiffer competition, and changing public tastes, do you have faith that your management team is ready to make the necessary organizational transformation to ensure that the company remains competitive?

◗ Does Your Company Have the Ability to Market Its Products?

Poor marketing and sales activities usually indicate that a company is stagnating. Do you think your company's ads on television or in the press are adequate? One employee of AT&T questioned whether he had made the right move in joining the company after he witnessed the marketing of its AT&T 6300 personal computer. He felt that the company was not aggressive enough in pushing this product in the already crowded personal computer field.

You may feel that it really isn't fair to judge your company by its advertising in the mass media, especially if your company is located in a very specialized field selling exclusively to wholesalers. In this case, you could always see if the company advertises in trade journals.

◗ Is Your Company Only Interested in Playing It Safe?

From your observations of management and your general impressions about the company itself, do you think that the organization has the tendency to stay within familiar territory and do business on safe ground? The best answer to this question will vary depending on the business your company is in. Some companies are situated in very predictable fields that require little innovation or new products. But if your company is in electronics, computer technology, or allied fields, a play-it-safe mentality can be lethal.

THE LEVEL OF EMPLOYEE MORALE

If your answers to the above questions have so far not given you a sure sense of whether your company is successful or not, perhaps you should begin to delve deeper into the workings of the organization. It is time to examine the social climate and morale of the organization.

The social climate can often influence how well a company will do over time, regardless of other factors. A good example of this is a football or baseball team with quality players, smart coaches, and a spend-happy owner that somehow never seems to win the big game and always seems to be playing below its potential. If you look closely at this type of organization, you will see that overall performance may be affected by something more subtle than personnel and materials at hand. Employee morale may be hurting the club on the field.

Here are some dimensions of climate you should look at in your organization to help you judge its prospects.

◗ Do You Sense Malaise or Joy Among the Employees?

The ability of your company to produce and succeed is affected by employee morale. What does it "feel" like to work in your company? Do the employees seem to enjoy their work or are they going through the motions, putting in their time until five o'clock? Is the average employee optimistic or pessimistic about the company's ability to accomplish its goals?

While these factors seem more obscure than balance sheets and marketing programs, their effect on the company is anything but vague. A company whose employees go through their day in a state of malaise, and seem to be marking time, is stagnating. This is not the type of work force that can produce the innovative ideas and exhibit the level of energy so necessary for the growth of a company.

▶ Do the People Feel That They Are Adequately Rewarded?

Nothing depresses employee morale more than the feeling that they are not getting rewarded for the jobs and functions that they are performing. Often organizations gradually become filled with workers who feel slighted, who believe that they are not receiving the pay, recognition, and promotions due them for the services they are rendering the company.

These people invariably develop into complainers whose main claim to fame is that they underproduce. If you sense that there is a widespread feeling among the employees that they are unappreciated and overlooked, you should begin asking yourself whether your company can remain competitive.

▶ Would You Consider This a Good Political Environment?

Usually accompanying, and perhaps the result of, malaise and resentment is a poor political environment. Backbiting, infighting, the development of cliques—all emerge from a poor organizational climate. You are probably well aware that politics is inseparable from organizational life. But a bad political environment, in which opposing cliques engage in ruthless encounters and glory in pyrrhic victories, can stymie organizational growth and improvement. It is not the best setting in which to develop your career.

THE EMPLOYEES' COMMITMENT TO THE ORGANIZATION

While politics and morale are important, you should also be concerned with your coworkers' level of commitment to your company and its goals. This factor can have a significant effect on your company's performance. Here are some questions you should be asking yourself:

▶ Are the Employees Fully Involved with the Job at Hand?

You can tell from your day-to-day interactions whether your coworkers are really concerned with the way the product turns out and whether they feel personally responsible for their work.

▶ Is There High Turnover in Your Company?

Committed people stay in their jobs; alienated workers eventually leave. It's as simple as that.

And the high turnover that results from lack of commitment has several implications for the company: It must increasingly get involved in training new people to do the job; it will lose the valued services of seasoned veterans; and it will have to suffer the low morale that results from high turnover. You must carefully evaluate your motivation for staying in a company that quite simply does not have the support of its workers.

YOUR COWORKERS' UNDERSTANDING OF THE COMPANY'S PURPOSE

You must consider more than the morale and commitment of your corporation's workers. Company fortunes quickly become undone when employees, regardless of their energy and motivation, never receive clear signals about the company's purpose or method of doing things.

▶ Are Projects Clearly Defined and Staff Clearly Assigned?

We've all known colleagues who seem to drift through their careers, always seeming to be on the fringe of the organization's activities, never really involved in the focal work at hand. Very often it is not the fault of the individual but of the organization, which never really clarified the role the person was to play in the organization.

Now think of an entire company adrift, where projects begin with no purpose and are summarily terminated with little explanation, where several often contradictory orders emerge from a variety of power factions and different levels of the hierarchy.

Does this seem like your organization?

▶ Are People Sure of Their Role in the Organization?

The best-run armies and ball teams are those in which people not only get explanations of the task at hand but are clearly told what their role in the task is. Do you notice that your fellow workers are confused about their roles? Once projects are initiated, do conflicts constantly emerge about territoriality, roles, rights, duties, and obligations? If this is a company-wide type of problem, beware.

◗ Do the Employees Seem Sure of How to Accomplish Your Organization's Goals?

Another question you should ask about your organization is whether it is instructing its personnel on how to go about performing their jobs. The first indication of strength in this area is the existence of company-wide training programs.

Also, you should be concerned about the extent to which the ordinary worker is ready and willing to help others learn their jobs. Companies and work units with a sense of cooperation and esprit de corps usually have members who are willing to help others perform their jobs, show them the ropes, and act as coaches, teachers, and mentors.

YOUR COMPANY'S PROPENSITY TO INNOVATE

You should really be wary of a company that has no interest in innovation and entrepreneurship. As mentioned earlier, in some fields this tendency can be devastating. But whatever your present company's field, it must innovate somewhat to continue to thrive. And if it doesn't look as though it is about to expand, you should begin considering other options.

◗ Does Your Company Support New Research?

A crucial indication of your company's propensity to innovate is the extent to which it supports research. Do top and middle management have a formal commitment to discovering new products, and are they willing to back this commitment with hard dollars invested in research?

Whether you work for an electronics firm or a financial institution, you should be concerned with your company's propensity to innovate. Even such a "low tech" services company as a bank should be able to innovate. For instance, since deregulation, many banks are breaking out of their "lending and borrowing" mold and are now offering services once restricted to brokerage firms, such as financial advice, investment counseling, and portfolio management.

While it may seem obvious that banks would automatically expand into these areas once regulation was lifted, you would be surprised how many banking institutions were happy to remain within the restricted world of conventional banking.

▶ Does Your Company Seem Hungry for New Ideas?

The suggestion box is considered outmoded by many organizations. But most progressive, successful companies, like the ones highlighted in the book *In Search of Excellence*, were quite interested in exploring new ideas, experimenting with them, and testing them in limited markets. Does your company seem to be this type of organization?

▶ Do New Ideas Get Committeed to Death?

This is important. Some companies pay lip service to new ideas but then let these ideas die in committee. The most progressive companies—the "excellent" companies highlighted by Peters and Waterman, and by Rosabeth Kantor in her book *The Changemasters* —made sure that new ideas, regardless of their source in the organization, managed to reach higher-ups so that they could at least be considered for implementation.

The really successful companies would even give the

idea-proposer, no matter what his or her level, money and personnel to pursue the idea. This propensity to innovate should certainly be a deciding factor in your decision to leave or not to leave.

Now that you have mentally explored your company's prospects for success, you can better ascertain whether you should seriously consider leaving. Of course, as mentioned before, if you bought this book, you already have an inkling that something could be wrong with the company. But hopefully, with the help of this chapter, you can ascertain whether you must make an emergency decision.

We asked questions about several aspects of your company. Most companies ordinarily emerge positively on some categories, negatively on others. What's important for you at this point is whether the mix of responses to these questions signifies that your company is successful or unsuccessful. You probably have begun to ask yourself some hard questions about the company's finances. And you are probably asking some questions about just how committed your coworkers are to the company and to the job.

If you are becoming convinced that your company is stagnating, has no place to go but down, and hence has no room for you to grow, don't wait for the inevitable to happen; don't become a victim of a layoff, termination, bankruptcy, or corporate contraction. Get your résumé out, begin reading want ads, and start going on interviews.

Are You on the Fast Track?

Now that you've settled in your mind the general condition of your company, you must turn your attention to an equally important consideration: your prospects of enjoying a successful career there. In this section you will find questions designed to help you determine if you are on the fast track—if you are making adequate progress up your company's career ladder.

We will look at a range of factors crucial to success in organizations: relationships with peers and superiors, rewards, recognition, and status. This should help sensitize you to some of the issues we will focus on in evaluating positions in other organizations, in future job offers.

THE STRENGTH OF YOUR RELATIONSHIP WITH SENIOR MANAGEMENT

You won't go very far in your organization if you do not have a good relationship with the powerful people there. These are the people who can determine how successful you will eventually be in the organization by promoting you and giving you the best assignments.

◆ Are You Friendly with the Higher-ups?

Politics is so important in any organization. It is a fact of modern corporate life that the careers of many managers and employees depend on their ability to "play the game." Whether you work in the mail room or occupy a middle management position, being known by top management and having that "top-of-mind awareness" is crucial to success in any organization.

Much of this recognition comes from social familiarity. When was the last time you went to lunch with the boss? Do you commute with some top managers? If you work in a small firm, are you known by the owner or partner? Are you on a first-name basis with the higher-ups?

▶ Are You Thought of Positively by the Powerful People in the Organization?

Do the senior managers or the owners of your company know your work and think highly of you? Most people approach their jobs with the belief that if they perform well somehow the information about their excellent work will reach the right people. Unfortunately, this is often simply not the case. It is possible to produce quality work and simultaneously maintain zero visibility with the people who count in the organization.

The people who do well are those who have managed to create an aura of competence around themselves, who have managed to acquire a quality reputation by working visibly. These are the people who become known by senior management as budding superstars and corporate winners.

A secretary in one large communications company gained the attention of one of the senior executives through her excellent work. He took an interest in her career and eventually had her promoted out of the ranks. She is now on a clerical track that can later lead to supervisory and management positions if she acquires the requisite degree. Certainly, in her case, being noticed by top management has dramatically improved her chances for success in the company.

◆ Do You Have a Mentor?

As I pointed out in *The Mentor Connection*, having a mentor is a sure sign that you are on the fast track. It can be one of the quickest ways to the top.

Do you have a mentor? This is a person who oversees the development of your career, who teaches and coaches you, who provides psychological counseling, and who runs political interference for you and, when possible, has a hand in your promotion. A mentor plays a powerful role in shaping your career and pushing you up the corporate ladder.

You should also be concerned about whether competing colleagues may have powerful mentors. One woman whom I interviewed, a second vice president of a large bank, was visibly upset when she was passed over for promotion. As it turns out, the man who did get the promotion was the protégé of the senior executive who had final say in who advanced in the company. As she put it, the two were "cozy" with each other, often having drinks together. The person who got this promotion—who stepped over the woman on his way to the top—obviously knew how to play the game of corporate politics.

We will deal with the role of mentoring in your career success throughout the book. The applications of this powerful tool to your career are endless. For now, suffice it to say that whether or not you have a mentor is a critical factor in your decision to leave or not to leave.

◆ Do You Work on the Most Important Projects in the Department?

One major chemical conglomerate I observed usually had several projects in operation at the same time. According to a young manager at the company, the priorities of the company were such that you could really divide the work into "A" projects and "B" projects. But only those with access to organizational intelligence really knew which projects were the most highly valued, the "A" projects.

Participation in core projects is a sure sign that you are on the fast track, especially since these serve as vehicles for you to rub elbows with the top managers and to demonstrate competence. Similarly, your absence from such projects could indicate that you should begin to look into other career options.

THE OPPORTUNITY TO ACCOMPLISH YOUR GOALS

There is nothing more frustrating than having good ideas and the ability to carry them out but at the same time being prevented from implementing them. Some companies are what I call failure-inducing organizations: They are set up in such a way as to frustrate their employees' attempts to utilize their abilities optimally.

The following questions should shed some light on whether your company is prone to induce you and others to fail:

▶ Are You Able to Communicate Your Ideas Upward?

Do your ideas for improving the way the company functions—the way it goes about marketing, researching, or producing its products—reach beyond your department, your division, or your level?

You will never move up the organizational ladder if you cannot transmit your ideas to the higher sectors of the organization. However, if the ideas you offer on new products or marketing techniques are regularly given serious consideration, you have a clear indication that your organization considers you a fast-tracker.

♦ Are You Given the Facilities to Implement Your Ideas?

Once your ideas are received by the powers that be, are you given the facilities, staff, and/or budget to make those ideas a reality?

This is an important issue in your decision to leave or stay. If you don't have the proper means to actualize your ideas, you may as well investigate your options. People at various levels of the hierarchy become frustrated at the inability to implement their ideas.

♦ Are You Receiving Training for Your Job?

An important component of being able to accomplish your goals is the organization's willingness to equip you with the skills necessary to perform your current job.

And training helps your career mobility in two ways. First, it helps you accomplish your goals and perform your job. Second, it indicates exactly how interested higher management is in your succeeding and acquiring a position of power in the organization. Participation in some training programs often marks the enrolled individual as a winner, a comer.

BEING REWARDED FOR A JOB WELL DONE

These questions deal with the most apparent indicators of success: rewards and recognition. When thinking about these questions, examine closely how the company's perks, pay, and promotions are doled out to your colleagues within your department and division.

◗ Are You Being Paid Enough?

Are you being paid sufficiently for what you do, for the amount of work and profit that you produce for the company? Most people develop an innate sense of the relationship between what they produce and their salary and are quick to recognize an inequity.

Are you getting as high a salary as others in your field, level, or grade? And, equally important, are you being compensated less for doing more than your co-workers? This is unlikely to be the first time such questions have crossed your mind, but it is important to review them while looking at the big picture.

No factor is more indicative of being on the fast track than pay, and that includes bonuses based on productivity, merit increases, and plain old raises.

◗ When Were You Last Promoted?

If you have not been promoted—if only within grade—in the last year, you must begin to investigate why. There could be several reasons.

It could be that the firm is simply not happy with your performance. If this is the case, you should have been given a formal evaluation. If you are given a poor rating and therefore denied promotion, begin to explore options immediately.

On the other hand, your failure to be promoted could be caused by lack of room at the top. This is the case in many firms, especially those that want to pare middle management and adopt a more streamlined look. But you should really find out *why* there is no room at the top, because it could portend lean times ahead for the corporation. It's hard to get on the fast track in a company facing a slowdown.

Your slow rise may also indicate that you have sunk into the corporate woodwork. In short, you are being overlooked for promotion because of a factor we mentioned a few pages ago—your lack of top-of-mind awareness among those in a position to help your career. It's not that you have made a bad impression, you have simply made no impression at all. In a large bureaucracy, this is tantamount to career stagnation.

Regardless of the reason you haven't been promoted recently, your decision to consider options should not be a hard one.

◆ Are You Satisfied with the Perks You Are Receiving?

Being the recipient of a large number of perks could be a good indicator that you are on the corporate fast track. Perks may include a bigger office, a secretary, a bigger staff, a company car, a sabbatical, or membership in a health club. (A fuller description of the variety of perks will appear in Chapter 4.)

You should be aware of how many perks your fellow workers are getting. Again, everything is relative. How important are status symbols in your organization? Most companies utilize these perks to indicate that the recipient is a budding corporate superstar. And senior management is telling those not receiving the company car, the bonus, and the bigger office that they aren't included in the company's promotion plans.

While perks alone do not indicate whether you are on the corporate fast track, in combination with pay and promotion they can serve as a guide to whether you should seriously consider leaving your company.

Companies use these goodies to tell employees that they are either valued employees or part of the furniture.

YOU AND YOUR BOSS

Often, employees begin to look for another job solely because of an inability to get along with the boss or because of a feeling that their career growth is being inhibited by their direct supervisor.

Your boss can affect your career in several ways, by making your job easier, helping you achieve your goals, and influencing your relationship with senior management. This relationship should be a major factor in your decision to leave or not to leave.

◆ Does Your Supervisor Advertise Your Accomplishments?

Whether you are a secretary, a clerical worker, or a middle manager, your direct supervisor can make or break you in an organization, making you look good or presenting you as an incompetent. Some people's careers never get off the ground simply because the supervisor refuses to allow them the room to grow, to perform well, and to gain visibility.

Is this your situation? Are you being stifled by a boss who is only interested in ensuring that his or her little part of the overall organization works well and performs efficiently? We have all observed this type of supervisor, and many of us have suffered at the hands of such stifling individuals.

If you cannot get out from under the thumb of a boss who refuses to allow you to expand your role in the organization, increase your level of responsibility, and attend meetings that will increase your visibility among senior management, then it is time for you to think about leaving.

♦ Do You Think Your Immediate Boss Is Threatened by You?

It happens all the time. The bright, young, articulate person—a manager, a secretary, or a clerical worker, for instance—suddenly appears, possessing new ideas and seemingly boundless energy, only to find that his or her every effort is blocked, sabotaged, and ultimately frustrated by the immediate supervisor.

Has this ever happened to you? Is this happening to you right now, in your current job situation? Is this why you are trying to find out how to make the right move?

More often than not, your supervisor acts in this contrary and uncooperative fashion because he or she is threatened by you. In such a situation, the very attributes that should make you a valued employee may work against you, by contrast showing how mediocre your supervisor is.

It is almost impossible to overcome the negative impact of a threatened supervisor. And becoming more productive, more of a shining star, will only provide a further threat. This can throw you further off the fast track.

Examine closely how your supervisor, boss, or direct manager treats, perceives, and interacts with you.

♦ Does Your Boss Take Credit for Your Accomplishments?

Almost as bad as a supervisor threatened by your accomplishments is one only too willing to take credit for them. Many superiors have derailed a potential fast-track manager by surreptitiously taking credit for the subordinate's excellent report or project.

You may be in the dark about your supervisor's actions. You may find out only too late that that good report you put together no longer has your byline on it and that it now has been "authored" by your supervisor.

One middle manager at a large communications company was flatly told by her supervisor that a report she had spent three weeks researching and writing was now going to be submitted under her supervisor's name. The implicit message was that if the middle manager went along with this plagiarism, the supervisor would somehow reward her at a later date. The middle manager felt coerced into agreeing to this act.

If you sense that your own work is being "adopted" by your supervisor, you should ask some serious questions about your future in your company. This person is not only abdicating his or her role as advertiser of your skills but subverting any chance you have of gaining visibility among senior management.

Of course, you could confront your supervisor over this inequitable situation, and you might possibly achieve some positive response. But, most likely, you would only further alienate and threaten this person. In this type of situation, it is best to face the fact that you should consider a career move.

THE AMOUNT OF POWER YOU HAVE

The decision to stay with or leave your current company also depends on the amount of power you have in the organization. Power in an organization involves any number of components: the ability to hire and fire, the freedom to propose projects, the ability to expand a department, and the right to make crucial company decisions are just a few.

This power may reside in your title, or it may emanate from special knowledge or expertise that you possess. Or it may originate in your own charismatic personality or leadership abilities.

But if you don't have power now and don't envision having it in the future, you are simply not on the fast track.

◆ Have You Been Given More Responsibility Lately?

Fast-trackers are usually given incremental increases in the amount of power they have. They may be given more authority in certain areas, be allowed to acquire a staff, or be given extra assistants to help them accomplish their jobs.

A fast-tracker invariably acquires more responsibility in key areas of the company. Is this your situation? Even if you are a secretary or clerical worker, there is always the possibility that you will have more say within your department. If you are a middle manager, have you been recently given an area of the operation for which you and you alone are responsible?

Lack of power is a sure sign that the organization is overlooking you in the overall promotion scheme.

◆ Are You Involved in Budgeting and Administrative Responsibilities?

One test of your power within your organization is the amount of budgeting and administrative responsibilities that you have. Many executives stress the fact that power lies in the ability to control and manipulate corporate finances. This does not mean that you have to be the treasurer or work in the accounting department. But it does mean that you should have some discretion to spend and allocate some amount of money—that you ought to be deciding the fate of some portion of the corporate kitty. In the modern organization, money is power, and the ability to decide in some small way how your organization will spend its money is a crucial indicator of your power.

YOUR RELATIONSHIP WITH YOUR PEERS

So far, we have considered your organizational success (and your decision to leave or not to leave) from the point of view of your relationship with those on higher rungs of the corporate ladder. But your relationship with peers and colleagues is equally important in determining your corporate success. Only if you have peer support can you consider yourself a fast-tracker.

▶ Do You Get Cooperation from Your Peers?

Many a career has been sabotaged by noncooperative peers. You probably have a pretty good idea whether you can depend on your colleagues to help you do your job, provide information when necessary, and even cover your back while you rectify an error.

Many protégés or budding corporate superstars have devised ways to gain the cooperation of their colleagues.

If you sense that your organization is a dog-eat-dog, overly competitive place to work, where people are just concerned about themselves and their own work, you should really have second thoughts about remaining there.

◗ *Do Your Peers Resent Your Accomplishments?*

Your peers can resent you for any number of reasons: your success, their failures, even personality clashes. Because of this resentment, you should be on guard for attempted sabotage.

There are organizations that generate a festering resentment at all levels, to the extent that no one is certain whom they can trust, work with, and turn to for advice. If you find yourself the object of peer resentment, realize that you are in a dangerous environment, one not conducive to career growth.

◗ *Do You Have Access to the Corporate Grapevine?*

Having a good relationship with your peers will give you access to the corporate grapevine. This web of information, the corporate gossip network, can serve you in a variety of ways: It can supply you with information regarding corporate shake-ups, changes in corporate priorities, and even news on hirings and firings.

This is why good peer relations mean so much to your eventual corporate success. These good relations give you access to the grapevine that can increase your chances of doing well in the organization. But if you are isolated from your peers, and hence from this information network, you are probably traveling through your organization like a ship without a rudder. The information revealed by these informal networks is priceless. Without it, you probably won't stay on the fast track.

Making Sense of It All

You must evaluate all the information that you gathered by answering the questions in this chapter. Only you can really assess whether the sum total of all the negative information about your job outweighs the positive. You should utilize these questions to analyze honestly whether you are on the fast track or headed for disaster.

In spite of the possibly contradictory feelings and impressions you may have after examining all the above factors and categories, there are some rules of thumb to make your decision easier. If either of the following two conditions exist, you should begin to search out new opportunities and seek new offers:

1. You are not on a fast track in the company.
2. You are on the fast track, but your company is stagnant.

How quickly you depart depends on how poorly your company is doing and how much you dislike your job.

It should be kept in mind that sometimes the decision to leave is influenced by factors falling outside some of the issues we discussed here. For instance, the decision to leave may not be due so much to the company's overall success or your position in the organization as the fact that you simply have outgrown the job. Some companies have no room for you to grow, no challenging new job or enriching position to offer you. Even the promotions may represent an equally boring work experience. This may be the greatest reason to leave.

The job may be interfering with your life-style, the corporate culture may no longer be to your liking, or you may be working too hard for the rewards you are receiving. People become disenchanted for any number of reasons.

In any event, this chapter may have made you think about your organization in a wholly different way. Perhaps you now know that you aren't doing as well as you thought. You saw yourself as a corporate winner, a budding superstar, but this fresh reading of your career path and your relationship to the organizational power structure has made you rethink your position and your place in the scheme of things.

If reading this chapter *has* made you aware of certain weaknesses in your company or your career, don't be forlorn! Use this new awareness to motivate yourself to think about your options, to take the first step in a crucial reevaluation of your job and your life.

While some think this process painful, you ought to consider it an adventure. After all, you have career options. But it is easy to get accustomed to unpleasant, dull, and unchallenging jobs, positions that offer you no prospect of success. Coming to grips with the fact that your situation is not the best of all possible worlds is often the first step in changing your job and your life. Without going through this process, you can't hope to make the right move.

However, even if you and your company have passed all tests with flying colors, you may still receive a tempting offer from another company. Whether you are satisfied with your current situation or not, you must have a way to assess all those future offers. The rest of the book is devoted to that very purpose.

CHAPTER 3

▶▶▶▶▶▶▶▶▶▶▶▶▶▶▶▶▶▶▶▶▶▶▶▶▶▶▶

In Search of the Excellent Company

Regardless of how smart, politically astute, and technically proficient you are, your ultimate success strongly depends on the quality of the organization you work for. A company that goes bankrupt hurts the career of the talented manager as well as the mediocre. If you join a company that cannot turn a profit, has neither the resources nor the imagination to expand, and cannot find new markets, it makes little difference how talented you are. This type of company will limit your future and undermine your quest for success.

Because a company's future should be your number one consideration when choosing a job, you must be able to evaluate accurately a prospective company's chances for success. You are already familiar with some evaluation techniques from the last chapter. Here we will look at much more in-depth ways to assess a company's future.

What aspects of a company most indicate whether it will succeed or fail? And where do you get this information? During the interview, how much can you ask about the company without turning off the interviewer? And should you automatically avoid a company in hot water because of a government lawsuit or citizens' environmental protest? These are some of the questions this chapter will help you to answer. Only when you learn how to answer them correctly can you be sure you are making the right move.

What to Look For

How can you tell if a company is successful? If you remember, in the last chapter certain key factors emerged as crucial in judging a company's current and potential success.

Your first concern should be the company's profitability. How is the company doing on the stock market? How long has it been showing a profit? If the corporation has been showing a loss for the last few months, is this because of its poor business practices or has it merely been investing heavily and deferring earnings in order to build the business? You should also look at its market share. Has this key indicator been going up or down?

A good indication of a company's growth potential is the number of acquisitions it has made in the last year. An aggressive organization looks to buy other companies in its field and in related areas. This could mean it will expand the amount of middle and upper management spots in the near future, thereby increasing your chances for success.

You should also keep an eye on whether other companies in the field intend to absorb your prospective employer. In unfriendly takeovers the purchasing company usually fires a good portion of the middle and senior managers and replaces them with its own. You don't want to take a position that will be eliminated within six months!

Quite often a good indicator of a successful company is location in a growth field. Some fields are stagnant, have very little future, and portend a slow-growth career for anyone joining it. Other fields are so hot that almost any company associated with them gets pulled along by their upward momentum. While it is a simple matter to spot a currently hot field, identifying future winners is not so easy. Companies in the biotechnology field were considered sure winners at one time, but environmental regulation and public-interest-group pressure have slowed the field's growth. Computer firms, especially those in software development, were thought of as sure-fire ventures, but even they have hit an unexpected trough. But the staid and stodgy world of banking, as it moves into the brave new world of financial services, has suddenly become explosive and innovative.

When judging a company's potential for success, look carefully at its top management. Biographies of top management often reveal much about the company's prospects. Is it top-heavy with "dead wood"? Do many of the officers have track records in other fields, other companies? Who are these people, anyway?

Any information you can get on employee turnover should also help you assess a company's success potential. The average turnover rate for all U.S. companies is in the 19–20 percent range. If people are quitting at a higher rate than that, it may indicate any number of negatives about the company—a low pay scale, a conservative promotion policy, or a poor long-term business prognosis. Examine closely the reasons for high employee turnover in your prospective company.

When assessing a company, you should consider any and all dimensions on which you evaluated your current company, including the potential effects of the overall economy.

Where to Find It

Now that you have a general idea of what you should be concerned about when evaluating a company, you ought to become familiar with the variety of sources of information about companies. As you will see, there are many information sources to help you assess the prospects of any company currently considering you for employment.

REPORTS, PERIODICALS, AND BOOKS

There are few secrets in American industry. While we frequently hear rumors about inside information and its misuses, for the most part the general picture of most companies' prospects gets publicly reported. And what companies won't divulge, the press uncovers. When trying to figure out whether your prospective company is a winner or a loser, the place where you should start is your library or newsstand.

◗ Moody's Industry Manuals

This is without doubt the most complete industry-by-industry financial report. There are five separate manuals—*Industrial*, *OTC Industrial*, *Public Utility*, *Transportation*, and *Bank and Finance*—and these books will tell you about your prospective employer's history, its size, its product, and its officers and their backgrounds.

There are two drawbacks. One is that to use these books properly as a source of information on a company's financial health, you will have to possess some skill in reading financial reports. The other is that these reports have scant data on companies' movement in terms of product development and policy direction.

Some related reference books are Dun and Bradstreet's *Million Dollar Directory* and Standard and Poor's *Corporation Records*.

◗ Annual Reports

These are companies' financial reports that are sent to stockholders. What makes them so valuable to you is that in these documents the company's board must make clear to all its stockholders—the mom-and-pop type of investor as well as the Wall Street broker—how well the company is doing and where it is going. Losses are usually clearly indicated (even if the accompanying prose tends to emphasize the "temporary nature" of such losses).

According to Tate Elder, outgoing president of Allied-Signal's new ventures division, you should read closely what the CEO's letter says about a company. It gives you an idea of the company's problems as well as its opportunities and offers insights into what industries the company is thinking of entering. As a job hunter you should comb the report to detect whether the division recruiting you is part of the company's growth plans.

◗ Proxy Statements

These and the 10K reports are sent not to the stockholders per se but to the Securities and Exchange Commission (SEC). They are addenda to the annual report described above. These documents will give you a true idea of the corporate balance sheet, and in addition they will list the money that the company is spending on executive compensation and perks. (You might even use this information in negotiating your own compensation package.)

The trick is getting your hands on a 10K report. They are available for examination at the regional offices of the SEC. If you can't get the information you require from other sources, it may be worth the investment in time and energy to hunt down the proxy statement.

◗ Dun and Bradstreet's Business Information Report

If you have a good relationship with your broker, ask him or her to get you a copy of this analytic report compiled by one of the most respected business analysis firms on Wall Street. While it may duplicate some of the information you receive from other sources, at least you will have the most up-to-date company data. After all, if brokers rely on this report to guide them when investing their clients' money, you can certainly depend on the "D and B" to help you locate a successful company.

This particular service gathers information on more

than 6 million U.S. companies and provides an easy-to-comprehend analysis of their financial condition, operation, and management. Some of this information is confidential.

▶ Dun's Employment Opportunities Directory

This is another source of information on a particular company that might be courting you. You can utilize this directory to discover a variety of aspects of a company's past, present, and future.

▶ Almanac of American Employers

This is an invaluable source of information about a company's finances and pay structure. Based on an employee poll of scores of corporations, this book can give you a worker's-eye view of a company's direction, its tendency toward innovation, and its overall prospects. Of course, this is not equivalent to a broker's view of the financial health of a company. But the impressions of employees, so often based on inside information and corporate rumors, can often guide you in your decision to take a job with a potential employer.

▶ Everybody's Business

Subtitled *An Irreverent Guide to Corporate America*, this publication by Moskowitz, Katz, and Levering gives you a "plain English" description of several key companies. Written in a humorous vein, it tells you about a company's history, its reputation among insiders, the background of its key personnel, where it is going, and its performance on the stock market. It also reports on how the public views the company. As we will see later in this chapter, negative public opinion can often help shut down a division of the company or lead to expensive lawsuits. Thus, it is important that you know what your prospective employer's public reputation is before you sign on.

The book's two drawbacks are that it hasn't been updated in a few years, Moskowitz having gone on to bigger and better things (he is the coauthor of *The 100 Best Companies to Work for in America*), and that much of the information is chatty and anecdotal. But it should be part of any job hunter's library.

◆ Trade Journals

Every industry has a journal or set of journals that cover the trends of companies in the field. They cover just about everything, from a company's new products and endeavors to who is running the show. These journals will always keep the savvy job hunter apprised of industry trends.

◆ Wall Street Journal

Whether you are a job hunter, investor, or someone who just wants to keep informed, you owe it to yourself to read this publication daily. Information about a company's performance, scandals among top management, and changes in the industry as a whole that you should know about before taking a position with the company are all there in the *Wall Street Journal*. This is a valuable tool in your job-hunting arsenal.

◆ Business Week

The popular business press will serve you well in assessing a potential employer. *Business Week* gives overall views of companies and industries and long-term trends in the field. The writers are excellent and the information is fresh and usually accurate. There are some other pop press periodicals, including *Inc.*, *Forbes*, *Fortune*, and *Savvy*, that you may want to become familiar with.

These magazines try to predict which companies are on the way up, and they are often a step ahead of a company's own employees in regard to information about layoffs and scandals. And if you are taking a job with a fairly new company, you can probably find some news you can use in one of these publications.

◆ Business Periodicals Index

This index lists by topic all articles that appear in a variety of business publications, and even suggests subtopics and related headings you may not have thought of but that relate to your search. For the job hunter trying to find out what the press has been saying about a particular company or industry, the *Business Periodicals Index* is invaluable. Merely look up a company's name and see if it has been mentioned recently. Then you can begin a thorough library search.

Other indexes that you may find useful in assessing a company's potential are the *Business Index* and *Predicasts F&S Index*.

USE A STOCKBROKER

You can use your broker to get the dope on a potential employer in much the same way as if you were about to buy stock in that company. As suggested earlier, a broker can get you information on a company that you probably cannot get yourself. And brokers will often have access to gossip and rumors on management changes, new investment policies, new products, and the company's overall prognosis. A broker can also

obtain for you the key investment reports (like the
10Ks mentioned earlier).

CONTACT THEIR BANKER

If you can find out who your prospective company's
banker is, you can surely discover some interesting
facts about the company. You can question the company's banker about its credit line and cash flow and
ask the bank how long the company has been a customer. You may receive a candid response, or you may
get a veiled answer. Either way, you can tell from the
bank's response just how stable the company is, how
enthusiastic the bank is about lending to and supporting this company, and the extent to which it will go out
on a financial limb for this company.

USE YOUR LIBRARIAN

He or she can direct you to the publications you need
to gain a deeper understanding of your prospective
company. You will find librarians to be most helpful.
Since their primary job is collecting and disseminating
information, they have to answer your questions. They
are truly information specialists, and many have mas-
tered the art of the "computer search," a shortcut
method of culling the myriad articles currently in existence on a variety of subjects, including the company
courting you.

If you cannot locate any of the publications that I
have mentioned, you should ask the librarian to assist
you. Most can cut several hours from your search for
information on the company in question.

TALK TO THE COMPANY'S CUSTOMERS

If you really want to know what the world thinks about your prospective company's success potential, talk to the customers who have business dealings with the organization. Several of my respondents who were applying for sales positions found this tactic especially helpful. Talking to the customers will help if you are looking for a position with a company.

If you have good professional networks, you shouldn't have problems gaining access to a company's customers. There are several questions you might want to ask in order to assess the company's success potential. How do the customers feel about the company? Will they continue to use its products, or do they feel that they and others are about to switch to another product? Are they pleased with the service support the company provides the customer once the product is sold? And does the company pay its bills on time?

LISTEN TO YOUR NETWORKS

Your contacts within both the profession and the target company may very well be the best source of information on the strengths and weaknesses of the company. You must listen closely to the messages you receive from your network about company X's financial status.

Once you know which company you are interested in joining, you can create networks where there were none before. For instance, you can get a copy of your high school or college directory and use as contacts people you know from school who are now working at the company. Informal contacts are usually pretty candid about a company's direction. Most headhunters will tell you to utilize people you know, even family members who may work for the company. If you are taking business courses, try to find out from professors and classmates what they know about the financial health of the company and its plans for growth.

The only caveat I would raise in regard to the gossip and hearsay emerging from your networks is that even people close to an industry or company can sometimes be wrong and know less about your prospective company's finances than an unaffiliated journalist who has a pipeline into the corporate boardroom.

Savvy job hunters know that there is no one best source of information. Your analysis of prospective companies should be based on a combination of trade journals, proxy reports if you can get them, rumors, networks, and the business press.

You should become an educated consumer when it comes to picking a company. We can never be 100 percent sure of a company's future, but we can increase the possibility that we are not picking a loser.

The New Company

Information on the IBMs, the Allieds, and the AT&Ts is quite accessible to those who know where to look. But what if you are being courted by a firm in one of those fluctuating fields, such as computer software or genetic engineering? You never know if you are being offered a chance to break in to the next Apple Computer Corporation or Genentech. Many new ventures never get off the ground, becoming sites of career disasters for those who left well-paying jobs in secure companies to take a risk with what they mistakenly thought was the next Hewlett-Packard.

How do you get the kind of information on the corporate newcomer's prospects that seemed so accessible when you were researching the well-established firms? Admittedly, it's not easy. Walter Sonyi of Goodrich and Sherwood, a well-respected New Jersey search firm, claims that going with a new company is always a risk. He likened taking a position with some new computer companies to a game of Russian roulette. That is why taking a job with this type of company involves knowing as much about your own values as you do about the company's financial potential.

You have to decide whether you're a risk-taker who can jump into something like this.

In other words, there is no way to assess with total certainty the potential of such a company. You should utilize networks, contacts, and other avenues of information before taking a position in one of these companies.

But what if all your research finally reveals what you suspected all along—that this company, while possessing a high potential for growth, also has a high chance of failure? Do you walk away from the situation and look for a more established firm? Not necessarily. As a young researcher, I was approached by a startup market research company that wanted me to leave a more established institution to join it at a higher salary with a better title. Going with such a company invariably meant taking a risk. The company had lots of contacts but few current clients, and management could give few assurances that the company would exist beyond the next year or two. What would make such a position tempting, however, was the company's willingness to consider me as a future potential partner in the enterprise.

Many new companies can offer you something few large established companies can—a chance to own a healthy piece of the company at some future time. What such companies can't give in terms of assurances of financial stability they can surely make up for in the potential rewards of part ownership.

If you should receive such an offer from an up-and-coming business, give it serious thought. A potential pot of gold may make it worth your while to take such a risky position.

Evaluating the Company in Trouble

Occasionally you will be courted by a company that meets most of the financial criteria of the successful company but nonetheless faces a nonfinancial crisis such as scandal, government investigation, or public outcry over its political policies or products. Every day we hear of companies getting into hot water.

The fact that a company is having such problems is no reason for you automatically to forsake it as a potential employer. Any decision you make about working there should be based not so much on whether the company has a problem as on what it is doing to ameliorate the situation.

General Electric, for one, though it has been plagued by bad press and poor morale resulting from its bribery scandal, is acting quickly to improve the situation. For instance, it is imposing more rigorous safeguards against employee wrongdoing. McDonnell

Douglas, Allied, and others started internal ethics courses after scandals hit. Other companies have initiated such actions as calling for the resignation of a top manager or managers to prove to the outside world and their own employees that they will act quickly against anyone involved in wrongdoing. These measures may not be a cure, but they are indications that the company in question is attempting to get back on the right track.

You must evaluate what effect a company's public scandal or lawsuit will have on your career if you decide to take a job there. Obviously, taking a job with a company accused by the government of bribery or sloppy and dangerous manufacturing techniques poses a moderate-to-high risk for the job hunter. You may have a hard time making a good impression or being noticed at all in a company whose morale is low and whose every move or deal is being scrutinized by government agencies, the public, and the media.

But if a company is handling its troubles correctly, its employees may be infused with a new sense of purpose, of making things right. Turbulence can sometimes open doors for the new manager. Very often a company treats employees hired after a scandal not only as new blood but as solutions to their problems. And the fact that old-timers are leaving and the hierarchy is being shaken up may mean that new positions are being created and new employees are good candidates to fill them.

During your interviews, you should be candid about your concerns. Many job hunters think they are being polite by ignoring this issue, or that they will ruin their chances of landing a job if they bring up such unpleasantnesses. Obviously, there is a proper time to address this issue. But one way or another, you must find out how the scandal will influence the operation of the company and your career.

If the interviewers are up front with you about the scandal or lawsuit, it could be a sign that the company is trying to confront the situation. A circuitous response, on the other hand, could signify that the company is facing extended problems and is in a quandary about how to solve them.

If you are seriously concerned about your career, think twice about joining a firm that will not come to terms with its scandal. It is desperate and probably unsure about how it wants to fill its ever-growing number of vacant positions.

KNOWING IF THIS COMPANY IS THE RIGHT MOVE

A company unable to handle a crisis can hurt your career in several ways. A company unable to separate itself from the effects of scandal or a lawsuit may limit your chances for advancement or, worse, have an atmosphere so volatile that you or anyone else can be fired quickly. A demoralized company can affect your sense of job satisfaction. And, on a more practical basis, a company that is not handling its crisis well is subject to a level of disorganization that can reduce your chance of getting advice, training, and cooperation in your day-to-day activities.

But how do you judge whether the company is adjusting to the crisis or scandal? You can often pick up not-so-subtle hints about company members' feelings about themselves. One employee of E. F. Hutton, during the check-kiting scandal that engulfed the company, stopped wearing his Hutton T-shirt when out jogging. During the 1970s oil crisis, accusations against Sun Oil of price manipulation and hoarding of supplies to run the price up led many of the company's employees to conceal their company identification at cocktail parties.

The company can avoid having its employees act like those of Hutton and Sun Oil if it has been smart enough not only to try to rectify its problems but to communicate its action to its employees. But before you seriously consider taking a position with a company in trouble, you must know that the company is looking for a way out of its problems and is staying afloat during the crisis. Here are some of the signs that tell you that the company is looking for a solution:

1. The employees are candid about the problem and not afraid to discuss it.
2. The company keeps its employees abreast of the problems.
3. The company informs the workers of the solutions to the problem, that the "problem is getting better."
4. It brings employees into the solution process.

If the company is doing any or all of the above, you can have more confidence that taking a job there is the right move. Johnson & Johnson faced a horrendous morale problem in various divisions of the company after the news became public that one of its products, Tylenol, had been injected with poison. The top brass were stunned for the first few days, and many employees fretted about their jobs. J & J took the type of action that should encourage any job hunter considering employment there. It immediately pulled the product off the market, and passed on to the press and the employees everything it knew or heard about the poisoning. The company reassured workers that it would confront the calamity directly, and it distributed to its hundreds of employees buttons that read "We're Coming Back." In short, the company responded to tragedy in the healthiest way possible.

Since most companies' scandals and problems receive widespread publicity, you can probably get advance notice on how the crisis is being handled. If you know people in the company, try to get a feel from them on how the crisis will influence your prospective job and the company in general.

According to many personnel directors, you can also use the interview to get a handle on how much the lawsuit or scandal will affect the company. Be direct in a nice way, without criticizing the company. One of my respondents very much wanted a position with a corporation that was unfortunately under investigation for defense contract fraud by the federal government. Here is how this person thinks you should handle this issue during the interview:

> Sit down and say to them, "How will this affect this particular division?" I asked them if the lawsuits would result in significant layoffs. I never asked this in the negative. I always proceeded as though they were doing the right thing.

If they are hooked on you as a candidate, you can most assuredly mention your misgivings regarding the company's problems.

Using the Interview to Evaluate a Company

The good business schools know that often the most reliable information about a company's prospects for success will emerge from the interview. That is why these schools usually coach their students for the interview and show them how to use it to become familiar with the company's history, needs, and finances.

How can you use the interview to get the company to reveal this type of information? According to Tate Elder, you should come in with specific rather than general questions. Instead of asking the interviewers "How are you doing?" or "How will you do in the next three to five years?" you should ask pointed questions about their products and market strategies. He feels that by posing specific questions you not only improve your chances of garnering information about the company, but you also demonstrate that you are a thorough person who has done his or her homework.

Others concur. Walter Sonyi of Goodrich and Sherwood claims that it is perfectly acceptable to ask the company "well-researched" questions about a range of issues related to company success. According to Sonyi, once you envision the interview as a two-way street, you will feel freer to ask the company the questions you must pose to find out about its future.

A good method of asking these questions in an unobtrusive way is to ask where you will fit in the overall plans of the company. By asking about career tracks, your opportunity to get involved in new ventures, and your chance to grow with the company, you will indirectly be receiving information about the organization's ability to expand and its plans for improvement.

Your prior research into the company will make this interviewing process easier, since your questions will be pointed, direct, concise, and relevant to the company's overall growth pattern. And if you are hesitant about being so direct, remember that you are demonstrating to the company that you know how to ask questions, take charge, and arrange your thoughts. You will be perceived as intelligent and forthright.

There is one warning, though. According to many personnel professionals, once you've gotten the answers to your direct questions, don't probe. The interviewers will tell you as much as they want to. Don't forget, this chapter describes an abundance of other sources which you can utilize to get this information. And the further down the screening process you get, the more cooperative the company should become in sharing financial and other data. Some companies will even send you a financial report if you request it.

THE WEAK DIVISION IN THE GOOD COMPANY

There is one particularly good reason you should be direct and candid during the interview. Often people research the company, find it to be growth-oriented and profitable, and therefore assume that they are choosing the right company. What they don't realize is that the division to which they are applying could be the one weak or bad one in an overall profitable operation.

Why, you might ask, would a company hire someone for a weak division, one that is probably going to be phased out? You would be surprised how often companies do this. Some personnel people admitted to me that they had hired people for jobs that were vulnerable to extinction and then laid off these new-comers after six months. It is a fact of life that even the divisions that may soon disappear or be sold off must in the meantime be staffed.

How do you know you haven't been interviewing for the one deficient division? Can you safeguard against signing aboard the *Titanic*? The answer is an unqualified yes, as long as you know how to gather information during the interview. You can ask questions like, "How does this division fit into the long-range, five-year plan?" The company may respond that in fact the particular division for which you are being hired is about to be phased out, but they have long-term plans for you outside this division. You can then ask them what specific position and division they have you targeted for.

In general, the more pointed your questions, the less likely the interviewers are to mislead you about the fate of the division for which you will be hired. But if you don't pin them down with your questions, the company—while not lying about its survival prospects —may not go out of its way to explain the division's future. If you question your interviewers directly, you have a better chance of getting at the truth and protecting yourself.

FINDING OUT WHAT A CUTBACK MEANS

At times companies, though not eliminating entire divisions, reduce staff through layoffs, attrition, forced retirements, and so on. The effect of such a cutback on a new employee is not always clear, because cutbacks mean different things in different companies.

Suppose you take a job with a company that has

just let go ten percent of its staff. Obviously, your own job could soon be in jeopardy. Since cutbacks are often done in phases, you could have the unfortunate experience of being part of the second phase. Personnel heads admit that this is a common occurrence. But they are quick to add that very often after the initial cutback in staff, companies stabilize and then begin to grow. If this is the case, taking a job in such a company would be a good career move.

So how do you know whether you should consider a position with such a company? How can you determine with reasonable certainty that current cutbacks will not affect your career there? The first thing you must do is ask the interviewers whether more cutbacks are coming, how many people will be let go, and in what areas. You should also try to pin them down on just how vulnerable you will be during this layoff.

Posing this question can do more than prevent you from making the wrong move. It can also help protect your job if you do go with this company and there is a subsequent layoff. I have witnessed numerous examples of people who had directly posed such questions and were told by personnel that their jobs would be safe. Some time later, perhaps six months after they were hired, they found themselves facing company cutbacks. Very often in this situation, the people who interviewed the workers found them other positions in the company. Why? Since the job hunters took the jobs in good faith because of the interviewers' guarantee of retention regardless of corporate layoffs, management felt obliged to make every effort to save these workers' jobs.

Of course, taking a position with a company going through layoffs is always risky. But, as we observed, layoffs can ultimately increase openings. Companies often get rid of people without eliminating all the positions these employees held. If you can get some guarantee that you will be a post-layoff survivor, your career ironically may be helped by taking a position with such an organization.

What most of us discover during our careers is that there are no totally safe companies, divisions, departments, or jobs. You can do the research necessary to confirm that the company does what it must to succeed, and the interviewers can be honest and informative. But no company, no matter how successful, can control the economy, political environment, or public taste. In the competitive world of modern American business, there are winners and losers. The job market is no different.

But, as we saw in this chapter, you can avoid the most obvious mistakes in your job hunt. Admittedly, there are no foolproof methods of choosing companies. But through meticulous research and common sense you can maximize your chances of finding a successful corporation that can help your career grow. When you join a successful company, you know you are making the right move.

CHAPTER 4

◆◆◆◆◆◆◆◆◆◆◆◆◆◆◆◆◆◆◆◆◆◆◆◆◆

Getting Your Just Rewards

Making the right move means not only correctly assessing the prospective company's chances for success; you must also be assured that you will be able to get your "just rewards" and have the opportunity to succeed. This chapter will deal with the full range and mix of rewards you should be concerned with—perks, pay, and the chance to move up the corporation's ladder. The thing to remember here is that whereas you have very little control over politics, the company's finances, corporate culture, the quality of the job, and many other factors examined in this book, through astute bargaining you can indeed affect your access to most of the goodies covered in this chapter. We will look at how to assess whether the compensation package offered by your prospective company adds up to a just reward.

Money Makes the World Go Round

People usually equate monetary compensation with salary. For too many people, their evaluation of their compensation package begins and ends with the amount of money they will make. Yet they would be well advised to look at the whole financial package offered by their prospective company before deciding whether to sign on. As we shall see, monetary compensation can take a variety of forms.

SALARY

It is a natural tendency to judge a position by the all-important take home figure. And why not? This aspect of the job can have an impact on the rest of your life —your standard of living, where you live, and your status in the community.

There are a few things you should understand about salary before we go any further. First, many fields have built-in limits on salary. It is well known, for instance, that you have a better chance of making a killing in advertising, stock brokering, and marketing than in banking and college teaching. Second, though you may find yourself attracted to the glamour fields, they often pay the worst. You may want to get into publishing, but realistically even some of the most prestigious titles in publishing do not carry a particularly weighty salary. Some of the more glamorous jobs in another media-centered industry, radio, pay scandalously low salaries. Disk jockeys, for instance, often earn well below what their fame and public notoriety would seem to warrant.

In any case, whatever your career objective, you should be armed with information on the going salaries in the field in general and the company you are applying to in particular. The following is a list of some of the best sources of information on salary ranges. Most of this information can be obtained at your newsstand, library, or book store.

▶ American Almanac of Jobs and Salaries

This particular publication is one of the most complete representations of the current salary structure in the United States. It covers jobs in the federal government, academia, the professions, and key white-collar positions, and even tells you how much employees in service industries—such as airline workers, brokers, magazine editors, and magazine workers—make. Here you can find what top executives in American industry make. These salaries and jobs are listed by rank.

It is a book of amazing detail. One aspect that recommends it is that the researchers have pored over all of the professional and trade journals to get this information. The one drawback is that current salaries may outdistance those mentioned in the book, which is updated only every year or so. But the authors wisely append to each chart its source, allowing the reader who needs more recent information to investigate further by contacting the particular source journal or association.

▶ The Book of Incomes

This book describes the salary structure in a variety of fields but is neither as complete nor as systematized as the *American Almanac of Jobs and Salaries*. Nevertheless, this work by Krefetz and Helms contains a good discussion of salaries.

◆ Mainstream Access Job Finder Series

Like the two books above, you can find this series in any general library's career section. These books, while giving you an idea of the salary structure of a given industry or profession, also provide an overview of the field itself. This is especially important to the neophyte job seeker who may have little knowledge of the variety of jobs within a field or of its salary structure. This series is mercifully candid about the future employment possibilities and income prospects within the fields. It deals with banking, energy, and other areas.

◆ Government Publications

The federal government puts out a variety of booklets on salary levels and often breaks the salaries down by field and geographic regions. I find that these are not as useful as other publications, mainly because the job categories (for example, service workers, professionals) are not specific enough to guide you through the maze of job titles that you will encounter in the real world.

◆ Macmillan Career Information Center

This series of books also accurately represents the salaries and growth potential of various fields. In tandem with the above publications, this series should give you an idea of what to ask for when negotiating your salary.

◆ The 100 Best Companies to Work for in America

This book, which is updated periodically, will give

you very general guidelines regarding the pay policy of some major corporations. While the book contains useful anecdotes about corporate culture and opportunities, it is too general in its descriptions and contains little specific salary information.

▶ Periodicals

For up-to-date information on who's making what, you may be better off utilizing such publications as *Inc.* or *Working Woman. Inc.* gives very accurate information on what the top executives, such as CEOs and COOs, are making in different regions of the country. While you may not yet be looking for a job in that part of the organizational hierarchy, it is always good to know what the very best make. *Working Woman* has an excellent annual salary survey, in which it reviews salaries by job and field for both men and women. This could be extremely useful to women, especially since the survey highlights those fields in which women's salaries are competitive with men's. *Fortune* regularly performs an executive and managerial salary survey.

Your best bet for accurate, up-to-date salary information may come from a variety of trade and professional journals. You can find most of these in local or business libraries.

▶ Headhunters and Employment Agencies

Many job hunters get a good idea of their worth on the job market by discussing salaries with placement professionals. Whereas salary may be the last item your prospective employer will bring up during an interview, money is a subject that headhunters and employment agencies discuss openly. Since they are acting

as your agent, they must be candid about salaries. Ask
them what you can expect based on your experience,
education, and current salary.

◗ Want Ads

The salaries in the classified section of a newspaper
may tend to be inflated. But they will at least give you
a feel for the range of salaries being paid to people in
your field with your experience.

◗ Friends in the Company

People already situated in the company you are tar-
geting may be the best source of information. These
people are already familiar with the salary structure of
the company, and their knowledge can serve as a general guideline for what you can ask.

◗ Professional Organizations

These networks serve several important functions.
Many people use other members to help them get jobs
and as a source of information on what people in their
field are earning. People who work in relative isolation, like consultants and writers, depend heavily on
professional groups to fill them in on the going rates
for services rendered. But regardless of your field, the
grapevine of any professional organization can serve as
a source of knowledge on salaries in the field.

◗ A Guide, Not a Ceiling

Regardless of their reliability, the aforementioned
references provide only salary guidelines. You should
never allow these rule-of-thumb approaches to place a
ceiling on your salary expectations and demands.
Many advisers will tell you first to estimate both how

much you need to live and how much you want to make. You should determine what salary level will help you get the things in life that you really want: a house, financial security, and education for your kids. Once you have determined that level, then you can begin to think about how much you should ask for. Job hunters that I interview are always amazed when they are able to negotiate for a figure much higher than the published going rate for that job. So don't let anything undermine your salary negotiation. Use the above references as a starting point in calculating your desired salary.

Raises

After a year on the job, there is nothing more disheartening than finding yourself making no more than when you started. Because a combination of inflation and changes in your material needs can quickly devalue your current salary, you must make sure that you will receive healthy and frequent raises. There are several issues you must settle before taking a position.

First, you must determine on what basis the company gives raises. Must you be promoted to get a substantial increase, or can you earn a good raise at the same title? The one way to determine this is to look at where the starting salary lies within your title's overall salary range. If you are starting at the top of the range, you will have to get promoted to see any real advance in compensation.

Second, you also must ascertain how often these increases are dispensed. You may not make real monetary progress if you are reviewed only once a year. You should find out if the company can grant you a special performance evaluation, say at midyear, which can then allow you to upgrade your salary more often than officially permitted.

Third, you should also ask whether these raises are automatic. You don't want to discover six months after you take the job that raises are based solely on performance. Find out at the interview whether this is the situation.

The fourth issue you must clarify is the amount of the raise. Many companies now grant as little as 5 percent or as much as 10 percent or more. Often there is a percentage range. Find out what circumstances influence this type of increase.

▶ Pay for Performance

According to many management consultants, corporations are increasingly linking employees' raises to their total productivity. It is one of the hottest management and labor trends around. These plans usually involve judging middle- or lower-level workers in much the same way their high-powered executive bosses are. They receive higher raises, bonuses, or prizes for meeting certain performance goals. In the most stringent pans, employees who don't measure up receive little or no pay raise or are even fired.

American industry is increasingly determining raises by one of these pay-for-performance or pay-for-productivity schemes. Hay Management Consultants' recent survey of 600 companies found that one-third intend to push pay-for-performance down the corporate ladder; about 11 percent have already done so.

There is also a surprising surge in the use of incentive bonuses for all sorts of workers.

Even the mighty General Motors Corporation has become a believer in the pay-for-productivity ethos. It will place all 110,000 of its North American salaried staff on this scheme and abandon the automatic cost-of-living adjustments. Such plans have been adopted by TRW, Honeywell, and Hewlett-Packard. The more competitive the field, the greater the chance that the company will try to pare down costs and increase output by linking final pay and bonuses to worker performance.

Since your raises may be greatly affected by this type of program, you must get specific details about how your prospective company administers the program and measures productivity. Here are some questions you must have the answers to before you take the job.

1. What are they measuring? If you are taking a job as a word processor, it is pretty obvious how your output is going to be measured: words per minute, number of documents, and so on. The company will probably be very straightforward about the measurement process. But in many jobs, performance can't be so easily measured. How does one measure management productivity, for instance? At the highest management levels, companies look at net profit, market share, and other factors and give out executive bonuses accordingly. But if you are a middle or lower manager, your output is much more nebulous: meetings, employee motivation and coaching, and conflict resolution. Are these intangibles going to count as part of your overall productivity? Pay-for-performance plans can't easily measure your subtle but valuable contributions.

2. *How are they measuring your output?* Companies differ in the ways they actually measure performance. Some companies leave it up to your supervisor to determine the value of your contribution. Some companies have tried to involve workers in performance evaluation. They have workers rate the performance of their peers, and then managers use these evaluations to schedule raises. The idea here is that workers should know each other's contributions better than a once-removed manager or supervisor. The question is whether these people will be objective in helping to deny a fellow worker a raise. The results are as yet not in.

3. *Is the measuring process threatening?* There are a few reasons employees are uncomfortable with pay-for-performance schemes. One is that computers and surveillance are too often components of the plan. Employees are rated on how many payments they process, words they type per minute, or new accounts they generate, all of which have to be measured by computer. And could you live with the intense observation that usually accompanies a pay-for-performance environment? If you take a customer-representative job, under a pay-for-performance scheme you could expect calls from company employees posing as customers.

Another reason you may find this method undesirable is the fact that under a pay-for-performance format, you won't receive any raises unless you specifically contribute to productivity. This type of scheme differs radically from the old method of granting raises, in which the employee was usually guaranteed an increase in salary, if only to meet inflation. Raises over and above that were usually merit increases based on performance.

If you are highly productive, this type of scheme can be a boon to you. But keep in mind that some companies do more than just restrict raises to punish low productivity. In BankAmerica's credit-card division, while the top performers receive large raises, the bottom 20 percent have a limited time in which to get out of this quintile or get out of the company. In 1985 BankAmerica sacked 6 percent of the division's work force under this plan.

In any event, you must be told exactly what your employer means by "productivity," how much of a reward you will get if you are productive, and what can be expected if you are classified as unproductive. And find out if you will be judged as an individual or as part of the group.

In spite of all these drawbacks, the pay-for-performance scheme is a gold mine many would never surrender. In a recent survey conducted by *Inc.* magazine, one construction company reported that a manager making $50,000 dollars a year could earn $30,000 more by meeting certain profit goals. The risk is that he could also get no raise. Still, keep in mind the potential rewards of such a scheme if your prospective company offers it.

EMPLOYEE OWNERSHIP

Salary, regardless of how it is measured, is only one way of calculating your just monetary rewards. Companies very often will offer you a piece of the company as an incentive to join. As I mentioned, smaller companies are noted for this practice. One U.S. construction company offers the project managers 5 percent stakes in some of the buildings the company puts up and will even lend them money to invest in the company. If you are offered a piece of your prospective company, seriously consider going with this company.

◗ Stock Options

Many companies will give you the opportunity to buy their stock at a "preferred" discounted price. These plans are so good that employees are very often hesitant to leave a company for another without such a plan. These stocks, bought well below market value, can accumulate into quite a nest egg and provide as much retirement security as the best pension plan.

You should carefully consider the plan, because it really can have an impact on your income. If you are highly placed, you will probably be given stock in the company just for signing on. Ask personnel if there is any limit to the number of shares you can purchase at this special rate. Many companies have such a limit to prevent employees from using the plan to make a killing.

PROFIT SHARING

Many companies will offer you such a plan. What these plans essentially offer is an accumulated income based on a set percentage of the company's profits. If this type of plan is offered, there are a few aspects you should have the company clarify. You want to know at what point you become "vested" in the program, and can actually lay claim to the money. Some companies stipulate that you have to be there five or ten years in order to be entitled to the money, even though you are nominally accumulating the money all that time.

Profit sharing often substitutes for or adjoins the pension plan. You want to know whether this profit-sharing plan will be considered the whole pension or just an addition to it. You also want clarified whether there are dividends to which you are entitled and whether they are paid to you or automatically reinvested for you.

THE SIGNING BONUS

There was a time when the only people offered signing bonuses were CEOs and general managers. But now companies are realizing that these attractive up-front cash offers can help the company capture fine talent at all levels. One of my respondents was offered $10,000 dollars to take a job that entailed an unattractive relocation. And she was only an upper-middle manager!

One search firm claimed that over 20 percent of its placements of middle managers involved signing bonuses. Although bonuses for board chairmen often exceed $1 million, you can more likely expect a bonus in the $10,000–$20,000 region if you are a prized middle manager.

THE SEVERANCE BONUS

The term "golden parachute" has made the issue of severance settlements quite controversial with the American public and especially with stockholders of major corporations. There was a time when companies would have a set formula for how much money their employees would receive when they quit or were fired (for example, a week's salary for every year worked).

But golden parachutes changed all that. Now companies pay their top officers prearranged settlements in the millions when they terminate them.

Unless you are a CEO or member of senior management, you will have to be a bit more humble in your severance settlement expectations. But because golden parachutes have become so popular, in effect they have "upped the ante" for middle managers.

You can often negotiate your severance settlement before you sign on. In fact, you should consider this proposed settlement part of your overall compensation package. Beyond the dollar amount of the settlement, there are several aspects of your termination you should attempt to negotiate. You should find out whether they will provide outplacement if you are fired and if they will let you stay on until you locate a suitable position. More and more companies are offering this type of service. The best time to approach the company about these issues is before you sign on. The better the severance agreement, the more you can be sure you are making the right move.

CONSULTING

The popular impression of the consultant is that of the self-employed maverick offering skills in computer programming, management training, marketing, and market research to the highest bidder.

But many full-time employees of major companies do consulting on the side. One type of organization, the university, provides professors with the credibility and visibility to consult with major corporations, often for quite lucrative fees. Others working for nonprofit and professional organizations consult to the outside.

And employees in the computer field are known to moonlight as systems analysts and programmers.

You should consider whether taking a job with a prospective company will enhance your ability to secure consulting assignments. All that expertise and experience you acquire on the job could make you a valued consultant outside the firm.

Keep in mind, though, that you may face a problem common to new employees, a de facto restriction on consulting. Many research companies, for instance, will force you to sign a noncompetitive agreement as a condition of employment. This agreement will usually require you to refrain from any consulting that could be considered a "conflict of interest"—that is, in conflict with your employer's interest. And you must often agree that if you leave the company you will not start a competing firm until a year after your termination.

The point here is that the skill and experience you will get by virtue of working for certain companies will increase your ability to do independent consulting. And this can lead to extra money in your pocket. But this advantage disappears if you are prohibited from consulting as a condition of employment. If you have concerns about this, you should ask personnel or the interviewers to explain to you any policies that apply.

FINANCIAL PLANNING

Assuming that you will get the money you want, how will you go about spending, investing, and saving it? With tax laws and compensation packages becoming ever more complex, it is no wonder people turn to financial planners to help them through this monetary maze.

Many companies are now engaging financial planners to help you make many of the decisions necessary to succeed in this complicated economic environment. These planners may be investment advisers, stockbrokers, lawyers, CPA firms, insurance companies, and others involved in this growing service business to help employees with their personal finances.

You should definitely inquire into whether financial advice is part of your perks package. Typically, a company may decide to provide to each of its top ten to fifteen executives a complete financial planning program. The next rung may receive help with income tax return preparation and tax-planning advice. Those lower down the ladder might receive an hour of private consultation on financial planning.

Here are some of the formal planning programs that may make taking a position with your prospective employer the right move.

1. Income tax return preparation and planning. The tax laws are changing constantly, and you should consider free tax preparation a valuable service. It may include providing you with someone who will fill out your tax return with you and possibly represent you if you are audited. This adviser could help you in areas in which you might be particularly unknowledgeable, such as tax shelters and deferred investments.

2. Long-range financial planning. This type of advice can prove invaluable. The program might include, among other things, advice on buying stocks, real estate, businesses and so on. As your income increases, you must be concerned with such issues as providing for your children's education and your retirement. A planner can also help you determine if your disability, medical, and casualty insurance coverages meet your needs.

3. *Estate planning.* Your company may pay for a financial adviser to perform liquidity analyses and make estate tax estimates for you. Would you know how to protect your estate from depletion by taxes? The financial adviser can open up to you the world of gifts, assets, transfers, and family trusts. At least you will know your family is protected should anything happen to you.

4. *Your retirement.* New tax laws will radically affect the worth of many retirement plans. You will need a great deal of advice to protect yourself in your golden years. An adviser can help you out with everything from IRA strategies to planning for specific retirement goals.

5. *Seminars.* Though we all would like our prospective employer to provide personalized financial planning, some companies offer only seminars. Often these are a supplement to individualized plans. Subjects of these seminars may include tax shelters, financing your child's education, stock option strategies, estate planning, and retirement planning. A seminar can last from one to several hours and may take place in a large group or in a more intimate setting. The smaller the better.

Your total compensation package is only as good as what you eventually do with this money. The above plans, in whatever combination provided by the company, can protect your money, make it grow, and enhance the value of the money you receive from the company. A corporation that offers you financial planning as a perk is actually offering you a better compensation package because they are helping you plan for the future. Plus, they are saving you the money it would cost to get this information on your own.

The Chance of Moving Up

As stated before, making the right move means more than receiving the salary you had your eye on. While you should care about the bottom-line figure associated with the job, remember that your raises and other compensation are usually related to your place on the organizational ladder. The higher up on the ladder you are, the more you will get.

How do you know with some degree of certainty that you are not moving into a dead-end job? No one can guarantee that you will escape such a situation. But there are steps you can take to assure that the job you are being offered promises to let you move up the company ladder and receive more of your just reward.

LOOK AT THE ORGANIZATIONAL CHART

You should ask the interviewer to show you an organizational chart. This chart will graphically represent the various divisions and departments and will typically include all positions from top to bottom, and give you an idea of where you fit into the scheme. How far are you from the top? How close are you to the bottom?

This chart will also give you a good idea of the various reporting relationships. You can then ask questions about whom you must go to for information, whom you must report to, and who has authority over whom.

KNOW HOW FAR YOU CAN GO IN THIS COMPANY

Now that you have a view of the organizational structure, you should ask the interviewer questions about your possibilities for advancement.

A good place to begin when discussing your advancement is the career ladder. Where do people in this position usually go after they have been here for awhile? You have seen the organizational chart and noticed that there are some positions open in senior management. Is there room at the top? Do people from your position usually go into these senior positions? And where are department heads and supervisors usually recruited from?

You would think that job applicants always ask these questions about promotion opportunities, but it is surprising how lax job hunters are on these points. One personnel head at a publishing company tells a story about the typical applicants for the administrative assistant position. Most applicants, new college graduates from top English departments, assumed that the position would lead to a spot as editor, a standard career track at other publishing houses. Because none of the applicants ever bothered to ask the right questions during the interview, however, they never found out that their assumptions were unfounded. The administrative assistant position was essentially a dead-end job. Most left it quite disappointed.

It is as much the applicant's responsibility to ask questions about the career ladder as it is the company's to explain it.

ASK WHY THE JOB IS OPEN

This may seem like an odd type of concern, but the answer to the question about why this job is open may tell you a lot about how far you can go in this company. Is the job open because the last person was promoted, was fired, or took a job with another company? If the person was fired you must know why. Of course, the person might have been incompetent. But the job may be impossible to perform and thus serve as a poor launching platform for promotion.

You should also inquire into why they are looking outside the company instead of inside. Is it that they don't have anyone qualified? What you are trying to find out is if this position, for whatever reason, is one that people within the company are shying away from. Again, there *are* such things as dead-end jobs.

FIND OUT HOW LONG IT WILL TAKE TO GET TO YOUR GOAL

Besides the career track, you should also be concerned about the amount of time it will take for you to get to a given point in the organization. One young researcher was promised by a marketing firm that he could expect at some point to become group head and then vice president. But after questioning people within the company, he realized he could reach vice president only if some top executive retired. In other words, he could not reach the top through his own merit and hard work. The organizational structure would undercut his career aspirations.

Remember: The length of time it takes you to reach the top depends strongly on a company's growth. A corporation that is sprouting divisions and departments left and right will provide you ample room to grow and progress. So, when contemplating your promotional possibilities, keep one eye on the career ladder and another on the many economic and market forces discussed in Chapter 3. Your career is heavily dependent on your employer's success and growth potential.

ARE THERE BUILT-IN LIMITS?

We like to think that people rise and fall in organizations because of their own abilities. We also feel comfortable imagining that discrimination based on race, religion, or sex is a relic of a distant past. While such conditions have been largely eliminated, we know just from statistical evidence alone that few women and blacks have reached the highest rungs of the modern corporation. On the other hand, their representation within most corporate levels has increased dramatically in the 1980s.

Still, if you are a member of one of these groups, there are some companies that will do a better job than others promoting you. (P&G, Federal Express, and General Electric are currently getting good press for their promotion of women into the upper echelons.) You can get information on these companies either through the grapevine or from select publications. Women, for instance, can find out from magazines like *Savvy* which companies are best at promoting women employees.

Limits on upward mobility do not affect just women and blacks. For instance, some U.S. subsidiaries of Japanese companies have a ceiling on how far Americans, regardless of their sex, can rise. Of course, you may think such limits on promotion are offset by the pay and prestige that working for a Sony or a Mitsubishi can offer. Still, it is important that you know the score before joining the team.

IS THERE A MENTOR FOR YOU IN THIS COMPANY?

If you have indications that someone in your prospective company could become your mentor, you should strongly consider taking a position there, all other things being equal. You may meet someone during the interview process with whom you seem to have much in common, who seems particularly interested in you as a person and as an employee. If this person brings you back for a second interview or seems to insinuate himself into the series of interviews you are having with various staff members, you may have a mentor in your future.

I have known job hunters who joined companies strictly because they suspected that some senior executive would serve as their champion: they know that mentoring is one of the quickest ways to the top.

Also find out if the company has a formal mentoring program. This can provide a quick way for you to link with a person who can help your career. Though such a program is usually implemented as a method to train and develop incoming personnel, more often than not it benefits participants politically and provides them with a sponsor who can move them quickly up the organizational ladder.

If you have a chance of developing a mentoring relationship in your prospective organization, going with the company is probably the right move.

The Wonderful World of Perks

So many people have a distorted view of the types of extras that go with the job. They think the company owes them a boat, a corporate jet, and a large office. True, someone somewhere is getting many of these perks. But for the most part, jobs offer good salaries and good promotional opportunities. Perks are extra.

There is almost no end to the number of perks that you can receive from a company. One of the favorite perks is the company car. Just the fact that you don't have to buy your own car for work purposes can add several thousand dollars to your annual income. The car may be accompanied by a company-reserved parking place.

But companies can offer all sorts of exotic perks to ensnare the best and the brightest. Expense accounts can dramatically enhance the quality of your life: You can eat at the best restaurants, travel first class, stay in good hotels. You can live the good life, at least during work time.

Some companies will provide you with legal consultation, personal security guards, at-home entertainment allowances, and tickets to concerts and the Superbowl. The company may provide you with various travel perks, including first-class air travel and spouse-travel benefits, and may even allow you to retain all the "frequent flyer" bonus points that you accrue on company business. This alone could be worth a trip to Hawaii.

So the list is almost endless. Some companies are even giving key employees turkeys on holidays, dinners, theater tickets, and other goodies.

Generally, perks are a secondary consideration when selecting a position. Salary and income considerations should come first, especially when you consider that your salary at the next job will be negotiated in terms of your income, not the perks you are receiving. Sometimes, though, a perk like a company car can tip the scales in favor of one job over another.

But there are some perks that are more than just a frill or a convenience. Some can, in fact, have a decided influence on how you are perceived in the company and hence on your career progress there. We will look at some of the perks and how they can affect you on the job.

YOUR OWN SPACE

Many companies have done away with fully enclosed offices for even their middle managers. But in most companies, space is still considered an important perk. More than just giving you privacy, a large office confers status and implies power. For instance, at Holiday Corporation, vice presidents get 300 square feet of office space and directors get 145 square feet. Both get windows and glass-enclosed offices. But those below them get only cubicles.

At AT&T, your corporate status is well advertised by your office. As you move up the corporate ladder, you go from a cubicle to an office to a corner office.

Since your career can be affected by where you are located in the building, you should attempt to see where you actually will be working. The Buffalo Organization of Social and Technological Innovation surveyed employees on what aspects of the office they thought conferred the greatest status and power on its inhabitants. Here are those aspects you should be most concerned about regarding your work space, ranked from most prestigious down to the least:

1. Size of the office
2. Location
    a. Corner
    b. Many windows
    c. Proximity to higher-ups
3. Amount of furniture
4. A door for privacy
5. Quality of furniture
6. Devices
    a. Telephones
    b. Computer terminals (though there is a controversy over whether this means the manager is moving up to the world of high tech or down to that of a secretary/clerical)
7. Personal articles
    a. Artworks
    b. Plants

You should really look at the above list to get a handle on where you will be in the organization's pecking order before you decide to take the job.

STAFF

I will deal later on with the important role a staff plays in your ability to complete your work successfully. Here, I will only mention in passing that the number of people you supervise, including a secretary, is more than a pragmatic concern. It becomes a symbol of the amount of power you have in your organization. It may sound Machiavellian, but having a private secretary is one of the great status symbols an organization can award you.

I once knew a department chairman at a major university who immediately established himself as a VIP by convincing the administration to grant him—in addition to the usual administrative secretary—an "assistant to the chairman," a second-in-command no other department head had. The fact that many people in the university quietly asked each other, "Who does he know?" only enhanced the chairman's status. People began to believe that he must indeed wield power and influence with the higher-ups to get this special assistant.

CLUB MEMBERSHIP

The Adolph Coors Company grants club membership to corporate officers. You should find out about the availability of club membership, because affiliation with a particular club will give you an opportunity to develop informal friendships and contacts and perhaps even acquire a mentor. Some companies like Georgia Pacific Corporation, Philip Morris, Inc., and Smith Barney pay the club dues of their senior officers.

If you want the complete lowdown on these extras that companies are offering, two books might be helpful. One is *Perks and Parachutes*, by John Tarrant. The other is James R. Baehler's *The Book of Perks*. Both describe in detail what one can realistically expect in terms of corporate extras.

The Changing World of Health Benefits

Many of us have a pretty clear picture of what we want in terms of health benefits: a good medical plan, an adequate dental plan, maybe even a plan to cover trips to a counselor or psychologist. But be aware that rising costs have changed what you can expect from your typical benefit package.

Employers' group medical payments have more than doubled since 1977, and the projected rise is in the area of 15 percent per year. Because of this, employers are offering a new type of benefit package— the so-called flexible, or cafeteria-style, benefit plan. Instead of a standard benefit package, your prospective employer may offer you a "spending account," which is based on your position in the company and your years of service. You then can select any benefit package you want: a comprehensive or minimal medical plan; life insurance; pension plan; dependent care; extra vacation; disability plans; dental, hearing, and eye coverage; and savings plans.

This type of plan can save you money because you can choose whatever benefits you want, like life insurance or disability, and ignore those benefits you don't need. What you must be aware of, however, is that some changes in benefit packages may require more expenditures on your part. A major trend is for employees to pay more of the out-of-pocket costs. Many companies are now either including deductibles in health insurance policies or raising the employees' current deductible. Recent studies have shown that companies are charging deductibles of anywhere from $100 to $700 on medical plans. The company may also offer you a coinsurance or copayment plan, in which you pay part of the medical expenses until a limit of "stop loss" has been reached. This limit varies for different companies from $500 to $2,000. Other companies are simply shifting a portion of the group health insurance premiums to the employee.

The point is that the day of getting a full package of employer-paid benefits is coming to a close. Employers either cannot afford or are simply unwilling to pay these benefits any longer. You should review medical benefits, the pension plan, and the life insurance program to make sure that you won't actually be taking a "cut" in salary after you finish paying for the benefits.

The Art of Negotiation

Now that you know what kind of salary and perks you deserve, how do you go about getting them? There are numerous theories about how to negotiate for one's just rewards. One executive warns that you should not negotiate until you have sold the company on yourself:

You're selling yourself, you're selling your talents. You've got to wait until the company's sold on you. Then you should let them know that money's important to you, that money's a motivator. It annoys me very much, especially when I'm dealing with young salespeople coming in, when they start right away asking me how the commission system works. I'm not even sure I want you yet! Wait until you're sure that I want you, and then you're in a much better negotiating position.

According to recruiters, the best time to discuss money is between "we must have you" and "we've got you." Once you know they want you, don't be afraid to discuss salary and perks. This personnel director feels that most companies will respect you more if you show that you know what you want.

The most important aspect of negotiating to remember is that you are in your best position to get what you want before you agree to take the job. You ought to bargain for every aspect of your compensation plan before you are an actual employee. Once you have the job, you lose your ultimate leverage—the ability to refuse the job. Once you are an employee, the company no longer has to add on to the package because they already have you. Thus, your perks and salary, your benefits and staff, should all be discussed and agreed on before you take the job.

WHEN BARGAINING FOR SALARY, AIM HIGH

Your dilemma as a job seeker is clear: If you ask for too high a salary, you may scare off the employer. If you ask for too little, they may give you the job, but you will feel that the offer is inadequate.

Studies have shown that those who aim high usually receive higher offers. According to psychologists at SUNY-Buffalo, the demands of applicants who asked for a larger salary were met, as long as their requests were not outrageous.

The issue is how much is considered normal. Many experts feel that if salary is a motivating issue in seeking a new job, you should not bother making a move unless you are offered a 25 percent increase. This is not a bad rule of thumb. If the company comes in lower, you can always refuse the offer or accept it if other perks are thrown into the overall package. If it comes to the point where you can't move the company off a low salary figure, start asking for more fringes.

But aim high. It will show that you consider yourself a worthy candidate and will increase their estimation of you. One principal of a noted executive search firm advises that before you walk into a negotiation, you should know the minimum salary you would accept. It should be based on your budgetary needs, your perceived market worth, and what your neighbor is making. You should also try to anticipate the maximum salary the company would offer. This latter figure can be obtained from the sources mentioned at the beginning of the chapter.

WHAT OTHERS ARE GETTING

A recent study looked at what executives want and eventually get in regard to salary and nonsalary compensation. While you shouldn't let this study limit your horizons, you will see that even the high and mighty among job seekers do not get everything they want.

The study claims that of 145 senior executives who accepted new jobs in 1985, only 29 percent of them won an up-front bonus (as against the 46 percent of those surveyed who wanted such a bonus). While most got annual performance bonuses, only half of those who wanted stock options actually received them. Most who wanted a company car or club membership got it. But these statistics indicate that these corporate heavy hitters, who should be the best negotiators, still had to give in on some issues when accepting a job.

EMPLOYMENT CONTRACTS: KNOWING WHAT YOU'RE GETTING

If you're lucky, you can get your just rewards rolled up into one ball of wax. The so-called employment contract, which sums up what you will get in terms of benefits, bonuses, salary, and perks, can serve as an ironclad defense against capricious changes in your package. Although upper-level managers were once the sole recipients of such contracts, lower-level managers are beginning to demand and get some form of written guarantee regarding their perks and benefits. And companies are increasingly coming to realize that to attract and keep the high-quality employee, they must offer them contracts.

These contracts vary in terms of their complexity and coverage. Some agreements are simple letters specifying employment terms and what happens if the executive is fired. Others are more formal documents reviewed by teams of lawyers. These may lay out job title, responsibilities, base salary, bonuses, perks, relocation arrangements, and severance terms.

The best time to ask for this type of contract is when the company first comes calling. The corporate recruiter or its intermediary, the headhunter, can be a good source of information regarding the firm's willingness to offer such a contract. The recruiter can often act as your intermediary in the negotiation. At a later stage you may have to utilize a lawyer or lawyers to review the provisions of the contract.

Why is a contract useful? Let's look at some of the just rewards that we discussed earlier. Suppose, for instance, that your raises will be determined by a pay-for-performance plan. We mentioned earlier that one of the dangers in such a scheme is that there may be uncertainty over how performance is defined and measured. An employment contract can provide a definitive statement that can prevent misunderstandings later on as to whether you fulfilled expectations and how much you should get paid for the work you have performed.

The contract may serve as a "golden parachute" and define severance or termination agreements. If fired, will you get six months' pay, twelve months' pay, or no pay? As mentioned earlier, many employees are covered by companywide policies (for example, one month's pay for one year's work). But if you want to improve on what is offered to the average employee, you may have to go the route of the employment contract.

Certainly, any employee ownership plan must be described in this type of contract. It would stipulate how much of the company you will own and list your liabilities in case of bankruptcy, default, or lawsuit.

You should be as cagey about negotiating this type of contract as you would any other. Many headhunters advise not to become a nitpicker who consistently renegotiates new "needs." You will be perceived as a second-guesser who cannot decide on your goals and needs. Decide beforehand on five or six "make or break" issues: salary, perhaps; severance agreements; employee ownership. You can clarify the secondary issues, for instance, vacation time, without letting them become central to the bargaining process. Companies get turned off when you move all over the place in your negotiations. Also, many recruiters repeatedly advise that you let the company win on a few minor issues. This makes you look conciliatory and reasonable.

Even if you don't get to the point of negotiating a contract, reviewing your priorities will sharpen your negotiating skills. You must realize that while you might not get an employment contract, you still must negotiate terms of employment. You will still have to get involved in the give-and-take of bargaining. By mentally reviewing those conditions you will negotiate during an employment contract discussion, you sharpen your skills and more clearly define your priorities, values, and conditions of employment.

CHAPTER 5

♦♦♦♦♦♦♦♦♦♦♦♦♦♦♦♦♦♦♦♦♦♦♦♦

Make Sure You Can Do the Job

You are investigating any number of companies and finally find the one that meets your expectations regarding salary, perks, and the corporate culture. After several interviews, you are finally informed by the company that you have been hired, and you start in your new position. As promised, the company is doing well, you are receiving the pay, perks, and benefits that you were told you would receive, and the company style is just to your liking.

The only problem is that you are failing miserably at the job! Is it your fault? Is it the company's? Why can't you perform the job as expected? What happened between your interview and the day you began working there?

Probably nothing. What is interfering with your job performance are conditions that were in place at the time you took the position. According to headhunters, many factors influence whether or not a job candidate can perform the job: the candidate's skills, the training afforded by the company, and resources that make the job easier. If any of these factors are absent, the job holder—whether a manager, salesperson, or computer programmer—is doomed.

The problem begins for any of us when we receive the proverbial "offer we can't refuse." A fast-track position, it pays well and seems to be what we would consider a satisfying job. Besides that, the job is located in a high-growth organization in an emerging field.

The only problem is that we are uncertain of our ability to do the job. The skills are beyond what we actually possess, and we are not sure that the company will really provide the resources such as staff and budget that will allow us to perform the job adequately. But we quickly sweep under the rug annoying little doubts about our ability to do the job. Because these doubts are inconvenient bits of information that only serve to undermine our belief that this is a good move, we ignore them.

But as we will see in this chapter, you ignore at your own peril doubts about your ability to do the job. Only when you can perform the job, only when the company will allow you to do well, can you consider a job the right move. In this chapter we will examine in depth the variety of aspects of the job and ourselves that can undermine job performance.

A CASE IN POINT

The case of Susan illustrates how certain factors can interfere with your ability to do a job. Susan has had a varied career. Originally a hairdresser, she decided to make the transition into more white-collar work. She began this transition by going into sales, first with a tire company and then with a mail-advertising company. She gradually moved into insurance selling.

Later, she decided that she would like to move into a broader category of selling, specifically into the area of financial services. She approached a company, the Midwest Financial Corporation (a fictitious name), which after several decades as an insurance company was beginning to rev up for a big sales promotion of its new financial services division. (Deregulation of the insurance industry had convinced its trustees that it would be more profitable to become a full-service financial services company.) New Jersey was the site of its pilot program.

Susan was among the over thirty new people hired. Many were just out of college and, like Susan, had no experience selling these financial services. The services included a full array of products, such as Ginnie and Fannie Maes, money markets, IRAs, and so on. Considering the amount of knowledge necessary to sell and service these products properly, it would seem logical for the company to provide constant training and logistic support for this new crew of salespeople. But, unfortunately, Susan and the others became victims of cultural, tactical, and political problems that made them unable to do their jobs properly.

Let's first look at the cultural problems. The company was staffed by a group of managers who were primarily insurance salesmen, totally unsure of their ability to handle this new type of job:

> Midwest said they had a game plan, but they really didn't. All they had running the company branch were insurance people. So their ideas weren't going to change. All their ideas were going to be insurance ideas. The corporation never called in financial planners.

So the insurance agents really never accepted the new corporate mission. The young people they hired, who were supposed to be the hub of the new financial-planning program, had no logistic support from above.

Shortcomings in the training program only exacerbated the situation. Susan and most of her incoming cohort of salespeople needed training in financial services. According to Susan, the company had promised full training in IRAs, real estate, limited partnerships, and so on—highly technical subjects that require lengthy study. Without this knowledge, the salesperson is lost. The "training" that was finally delivered to the fledgling financial planners was done by salespeople from different companies. These representatives were knowledgeable only about the particular product they represented, like Fannie Maes, and were more concerned with pushing their products than properly training the staff.

Midwest did encourage the new employees, including Susan, to acquire training, but on their own time and at their own expense. For example, she once had to take a week off from work to attend a series of classes to attempt to pass the stockbroker's license exam. The company would reimburse her if and when she passed the exam. And not only was she out the money for the course, she also sacrificed a week of work. (Since she was on a draw, she was paid only when she was actually selling.)

Poor training affected her sales technique and ultimately her sales. She would constantly have to interrupt her meetings with clients to check back with her manager on the details of a particular plan: "My manager knew less than I did—and his superiors knew less than him." Nobody had a handle on the services. Her sales calls became a string of sessions in which she would have to camouflage her lack of training: "I would basically fake my way through the interview and then take the information back to the office."

One of the managers was actually a CPA who had some knowledge of the financial services now offered by Midwest. But this manager's time would be stretched thin trying to help Susan and all the others decipher what the products were and how they could meet the customers' needs.

Compounding Susan's job problems was the fact that the company never delivered the leads promised at the interview. These leads were supposed to come in two forms. First the company was supposed to provide all new salespeople with lists of customers who were already doing business with the company and could be approached by the new salespeople. The second source would have been seminars the company was going to hold for the employees of various companies and institutions. At such seminars the company would try to sell the attending employees on Midwest's financial expertise. But the customer lists and seminars never materialized, and Susan and the other new recruits were left to fend for themselves.

As if these problems weren't enough, the company provided neither technical nor staff support for the new people. To accurately do the financial profiles of prospective customers, the salespeople needed access to a computer. Since the company had exactly one terminal in use for all the new salespeople, each had to compete with the others for computer time. They also had to compete with the secretary, who used the terminal for word processing. To add insult to injury, this secretary was not permitted to perform any clerical services for the sales force. If the new salespeople wanted a clerical to do typing or send out letters to prospects, they were advised by branch management to "pool their resources" and hire a temp for the day —at their own expense!

The end result was a disaster. The parent company, treating this New Jersey branch as a profit center, wanted quick results. The parent put pressure on the managers for bottom-line results, but according to Susan this just made a bad situation worse. The branch managers, uncomfortable with the financial services products, began increasingly to revert to their real expertise, insurance. But they continued to represent themselves to new customers as a financial services company and lost these customers when the prospective buyers realized that they were being sent not "investment counselors" but insurance salespeople.

The combination of lack of training, poor technical support, and unknowledgeable managers took its toll. After eight months, only three of the original salespeople were still employed by the company, and the financial services experiment was in shambles.

How could Midwest have helped Susan succeed?

According to her, they would have had to adopt a totally different approach: "They should have hired us, strictly paid us for six months, with no sales. Paid us to go to school, to learn, to train, to go out with salespeople."

Does the above story seem like a nightmare, a career anomaly that just couldn't happen to you? Actually, Susan's case illustrates how any number of factors can undermine your ability to do the job and thereby sabotage your career. In this chapter, we will explore in detail the various factors that can affect your ability to do the job. In this way you will know before you take a job whether you will be able to perform it.

Only when you are certain that you can do the job you are hired for do you know that you are making the right move.

You Can't Do the Job Without the Skills

To determine if you can do the job you must first consider whether you possess the required skills. Most of us tend to assume that even if we don't have the requisite skills we can acquire them on the job. Later on we are troubled to discover that the company expected us already to have most of the skills before we took the job and is therefore offering little help in acquiring them.

Though the required skills are usually specifically listed in the job description, we tend to think that anything we lack in that regard will be taught us. In a sense, we put too much faith in the judgment of those doing the interviewing and hiring. We reason that if they think we can do the job, we must be able to deliver. But this is not always the case. Sometimes we get hired not because of our qualifications but because of our ability to sell ourselves. In the process we tend to convince ourselves along with the interviewer of our ability to perform. This is often the beginning of a career disaster!

Although Susan possessed both a basic ability to communicate with people and an understanding of their financial needs, she needed technical training. Assuming that she would acquire all the other skills through a combination of on-the-job training and learning by doing, she took the job. She also believed she would be given the time to acquire those skills. Unfortunately, she was wrong on all counts.

KNOW WHAT IS EXPECTED OF YOU

The only way really to know what skills are required for a job is to secure at the outset a clear understanding of what is expected of you and your performance. You should be candid with your interviewers and let them know that you want to know what they expect you to accomplish. What are the limits of your responsibilities? What projects will you have to have completed and by what date? Are all these responsibilities explicit, or is there an unspoken understanding about what you are supposed to accomplish? It is imperative that you find out before you take the job just what projects are under way and what your role will be in these projects. Ask for a short history of these projects and programs, where they failed and how they succeeded. This may be the only way for you actually to assess the level of skill and proficiency needed for a job.

According to Carol Aloisi, an executive with Johnson & Johnson, you should always try to clarify expectations regarding your performance. If you are a salesperson, find out when they expect you to make your first sales and at what point you are to come up to full speed. You should try to get the company to articulate specifically the sales objectives for the next six months, the next year.

She emphasizes that you must know when your first real evaluation will take place. In this way you get the company to sign on to a "psychological contract" regarding your performance. People just don't do that enough when they consider a position.

Don't be afraid to ask interviewers what the exact nature of the job is. Find out what the typical day is like. Several people I interviewed for this book mentioned that if the company does not object, you should try to interview the person who just had your job. One respondent remarked that she was encouraged to make an intracompany transition from personnel to sales by the rosy picture of the job that she received from the incumbent.

Ms. Aloisi warns that you must be honest about the fit between your skills and the job's requirements. If you don't have the skills, say so. This can prevent a later career disaster. Of course, there is a right way and a wrong way to approach the company on this issue: "You sell yourself on your strengths, but you say 'However, for your particular system, this is what I am going to need to know, and this is the help I will need.'"

THE REQUISITE SKILLS

But before we talk about how a company can help you meet their skill requirements, let's address the issue of your responsibility in this area.

The best way to assure that you meet the skill requirements is to take care of business before you pursue this particular job. While you may not know what a particular job requires before you walk into the interview, you probably know what skill and educational levels are generally needed for advancement in your field. That is why you must constantly keep your skills sharp.

If you think you will need an MBA to advance in your career, don't put off getting it. Also, you should keep up to date in your field. Since your knowledge of the trends, technology, and developments in your specialty can quickly become obsolete, don't hesitate to take seminars that cover the latest developments. These seminars look good on your résumé and impress employers who are always looking for sharp people.

Remember, although your lack of skills will inhibit your ability to perform a job, it is the most easily "controllable" variable in the success quotient. By sharpening your skills and increasing your education, you can ensure that a job that you consider the right move will be accessible.

Training Is the Key to Success

If you don't have the skills to do the job when you take the position, you will have to find other ways to ensure that you can do the job. Once you are honest with yourself and the company about any lack of skills you may have, the next step is to ascertain how you will make up for any deficiencies.

Some companies are very big on training, whether formal or informal. They assume that you don't yet have all the skills to perform the role you are hired to fill and that training will be necessary to hone your skills and bring you up to speed. But if the company you are considering does not provide such training, the chances are that you will fail.

Once you are assured that the company is willing to train you to compensate for whatever skill or experience deficiencies you have, there are four major questions that must be answered:

1. What are the new skills that you must acquire to perform the job adequately?
2. How will you acquire the skills?
3. How long do you have to acquire these skills?
4. What are the specifics of the training program?

Companies do different things to improve the skills of their employees. You must be absolutely certain of the education-training programs existing in the company before you take the job. Since lack of skills is a major reason for failing in a job, you must note carefully the variety of techniques the company uses to train and develop its employees and managers. If the company is vague on this issue during the interview, it might mean that training is desultory, capricious, or nonexistent. Beware of the company that pays lip service to employee development but offers no specific details of its training program.

Different jobs require different training. A particular clerical job might require on-the-job training, while a management position may involve eventually going for an MBA. Many companies feel that the only real way to train and mold a manager is through job rotation, which allows the trainee to experience for limited periods all aspects of the company.

You will feel more assured that taking a job with a company is the right move if you know you will receive the training to help you achieve peak job performance. To help you evaluate training programs, we will explore the two basic ways that companies upgrade the skills of their employees—on-the-job training and off-site education.

ON-THE-JOB TRAINING

Most of us acquire our skills at the worksite. But before you assume the position you must find out whether the training you will receive ensures that you will succeed in the position. Usually companies promise that this training will come from one of several sources—the incumbent in the job, your manager or supervisor, a peer staff member, or an outside trainer. Let's look at the different sources of training and the extent to which they can help you do your job.

◗ Your Manager

One respondent tells a story about a salesman who was hired for a product manager position by a new vice president. Although the salesman had never worked in product management, his extensive experience selling the particular product supposedly qualified him for the new position. The new vice president told the salesman that he shouldn't worry about failing in this new role. "I'll teach you everything you have to know," the VP proclaimed.

Unfortunately, the vice president was also just learning the ropes, just coming up to speed learning how things got done in the huge conglomerate. To make matters worse, another person was promoted up through the ranks to a position between the two men, further weakening the training relationship between the PM and VP. In effect, the new product manager was left hanging in the wind. His predictably poor performance warranted being let go within three months of his hiring.

The warning is clear: If the person who is supposed to train you is your manager or supervisor, make sure he or she has the time and resources to devote to your training. Even if the company is totally committed to it at the time of the interview, a new employee's training is often lost in the shuffle. Get specifics!

Increasingly, companies aren't leaving employee development to chance. They are encouraging their senior and upper-level managers to get more actively involved in training those lower in the hierarchy. Thousands of companies in the United States and elsewhere are utilizing formal mentoring programs as a method of ensuring that new entrants will do their job successfully. One medium-size consulting company assigns a project manager to each consultant. Each mentor is responsible for that specific employee's development and handles the protégé's problems, answering his or her questions, providing technical support, and the like.

▶ Peers and Colleagues

If a company cannot provide you with a manager or

supervisor to bring you up to speed, they may intend that you be trained by peers or colleagues. While this method is helpful, you should clarify at the interview which coequal will have final responsibility for your training. Many a career has been dashed because companies have left the training of new-entry peers to chance.

Try to ascertain at the interview not only who will be doing the training but whether they have time and knowledge to improve your skills. Keep in mind that if you fail, the company will most likely not blame its own shortcomings in the training area. It will just decide that it made the wrong decision in hiring you in the first place.

Some companies that use job rotation as a form of training involve the new recruits' colleagues in the process. For instance, Wakefern, the co-op representing the ShopRite stores, makes sure that new recruits are placed in a variety of company settings to gain exposure to the company's day-to-day operations before they assume managerial positions. One sales trainee in a large pharmaceutical firm was allowed to spend a day in one of the company's labs to experience sales from the customers' viewpoint. She interfaced with salespeople to get a feel for her own job.

▶ The Incumbent

The job incumbent can provide some of your most effective training during the early period of your tenure. Because this person's experience is invaluable, it is not unheard of for new jobholders to insist that the company let them be trained by the person who used to have the job.

If the company is willing to meet this demand, you

should find out how long you will have with the person. A few days with the job incumbent will provide you with a smooth transition into the new position.

▶ The Consultant

Some companies realize that they will not be able directly to provide adequate training to get you up to speed in day-to-day operations. In such cases they may allow you to hire a consultant to help you learn the job. You should attempt to clarify early on whether you will be able to hire one or more people to advise, counsel, and train you for your new position.

At one point in her career, one of my respondents took a human resources position that required her to deal with affirmative action plans much more complex than those she was accustomed to. Aside from this one minor problem, the job had all the pay and perks ingredients of the right move. "So when I went I explained that I understood the laws and affirmative action very well. I understood the basics. But I did not know this particular company, so what could they expect?"

Since the company knew that she was superb for the job but lacked certain skills necessary for performing affirmative action audits for Fortune 500 companies, a compromise was reached. The firm allowed her to hire a consultant who had worked with Fortune 500 companies to train her in this one area.

OFF-SITE EDUCATION

The alternative to on-site training is education at an institution or school. Many companies assume that you have certain deficiencies that can be eliminated only through a variety of formal methods, including degree programs and seminars.

◆ When Taking the Job Means Going Back to School

Some companies are very blunt about it. You must get another degree to be able to function in the job. They hire you under the assumption that you will go for further schooling.

The first issue you must confront is whether you want to take a job that requires further schooling. Extra degrees mean a considerable investment of time, money, and energy. Let's look at some of these factors to see if a company that requires further education adds up to the right move.

Education takes *time*. Many new managers are encouraged to go for an MBA, which can take two or more years to complete. Will the company give you time off from work to attend late-afternoon or early-evening classes? If the firm really wants you, it may even offer to send you to one of those six-month, full-time programs administered by some universities. That means time away from work.

The next issue is money. If they are so intent on having you acquire the extra degree, are they willing to pay for it? If they are vague about how much they will contribute to your degree, don't rush into the job.

You must also examine your own desire to add to the amount of time you have already spent in school. Approach the job from a cost-benefit standpoint. You will have to put a substantial amount of physical and mental energy into the process: You will have to transport yourself to the school, sit in classes, and study on weekends. Even if you have the time to go for the degree and the company will assume all costs, you must still have the motivation and energy to complete the degree. Your motivation becomes especially relevant if your prospective employer places a time limit on attaining the degree. You will not only have to go for the BA or MBA but will have to do so within so many years. This could involve sacrificing your summers to complete the degree quickly.

These factors may convince you that you don't want to join a company that requires you to go back to school in order to perform your job well. In this situation, only if you are prepared to put in the time and expend the energy for one more degree can you consider going with this company the right move.

◗ Less Painful Formal Educational Programs

Fortunately, most companies enhance your ability to do the job through seminars and one-shot courses. At AT&T, any employee can attend one- to two-week courses on everything from cellular communications to marketing techniques. Other companies sharpen employees' supervisory skills by sending them out to three-day management development seminars.

A growing number of companies realize that while further degrees are nice, the employee's ability to perform his or her job can be improved by short courses targeted to the employee's weak points. Do you lack presentation skills? Do you have problems writing a memo? Do you have a problem confronting subordinates? Do you want to enhance your ability to appraise your employees' performance? There are courses to help you in all these areas. You must find out in the interview whether the company has any regular program for enhancing your skills.

Generally, you can feel more confident if a company

has a policy that mandates employee training on a regular basis by professional on-staff trainers or consultants in the field. Ask at the interview. Also ask to see a copy of the employee newsletter. Many companies feature news about upcoming seminars in these monthly newsletters, a good indication that they are dedicated to keeping the employees well trained and productive.

When trying to assess whether going with a company is the right move, remember that you can only succeed when the company allows you to function well. Training, whether on-site or more formalized, is basic to your ability to do the job.

Power

The skills you bring to the job and the training you receive later on are not the only determinants of your ability to reach peak job performance. Organizational and political factors are equally important. One of the most important of these is your total amount of organizational power.

You might be thinking of leaving your current job because you recognize the fact that your lack of power is undermining your effectiveness. In my research I regularly encounter people who are not given any real power to accomplish the goals their job supposedly mandates.

I once new a chairman of a college department who had been brought in by the university president to help develop a new business school out of a good but sleepy management department. His mandate was to hire new faculty, create new courses, and give the department a new direction. But the chairman's authority turned out to be insufficient for overcoming the resistance of the tenured senior faculty who had a vested interest in the status quo. Most of these tenured professors had little interest in being part of the new business school, so they resisted the chairman's efforts at every turn and sabotaged his grand scheme. In the classic sense, he had formal authority but little real *power*.

Another example is a woman I recently interviewed who was brought into a large communications company in a marketing capacity. Since the company was only recently forced by government dictum to become more competitive, they needed someone to help the company become more marketing-oriented. Unfortunately, the company's top management, itself unfamiliar with the role of the marketing executive, handed her a lofty title but little decision-making power over pricing, shipping, distribution, or any of the other aspects of the marketing job. When it became obvious to her that territories had to be reallocated and prices revamped, she realized that the company had given her no authority to change the sales patterns (or to fire the salespeople). The sales staff, sensing her lack of real power, was in constant rebellion, and for two years she literally had to harass them before she could get them even to begin to cooperate with her overall marketing plans. The company had failed to give her the authority to make de facto decisions in regard to pricing and distribution routes. She had position but little power. Like the new chairman, she could not do her job.

To avoid these problems, and to make sure that you have sufficient power to be able to do the job you are hired for, you should get answers to the following questions.

HOW MUCH POWER ARE THEY ACTUALLY GIVING YOU?

Ask to see your job description. These few paragraphs will tell you exactly how much power you have to accomplish the stated goals. They give you formal authority to order this person and that person to do tasks X and Y. If you do not come to an explicit understanding regarding your formal authority before you take the job, don't be surprised later on at your inability to do the job you were hired to do.

HOW MUCH POWER DOES YOUR SUPERVISOR HAVE?

Often your ability to do a job is determined by your supervisor's power over the rest of the organization. In other words, your supervisor's power is your power. Since you will be interviewed by the person who most likely will be your supervisor, try to get a handle on how many organizational resources are controlled by that person, how large a staff that person has. Ask that person to describe his or her role in recent projects.

Time and experience will sharpen your ability to analyze power situations. When asked directly, most people will tell you that they have enormous power and influence in their department and organization. Separating fact from fiction in a supervisor's version of corporate reality is not an easy process. But if you can't get an accurate reading of your supervisor's organizational power, you may be taking the job with unreasonably high expectations about your ability to do it.

IS THE SUPERVISOR READY TO DELEGATE AND SHARE POWER?

You can only do your job correctly if you are given freedom to act independently. There is no greater hindrance to job performance than being required to check with your manager every time you want to make a decision. Try to find out during the interview how much latitude you will have in executing your decisions. Try to find out how power will be divided or shared between you and your immediate boss. Only when you know that you have the freedom to act with some degree of autonomy do you know that you are making the right move.

CAN YOU GET YOUR IDEAS HEARD?

If the higher-ups don't listen to your ideas, you are in a poorer position to do your job. This is because very often you are the only person who knows the problems that emerge in the day-to-day performance of your job. You must be able to sensitize your immediate boss and the higher-ups to the changes that are taking place that affect how you do your job. If they are insensitive to your ideas, you will fail.

For example, you may be a salesman who needs extra support or more rapid delivery of products. You may be a manager who thinks that you need a larger or better trained staff. Whatever your needs, if you don't have the ability to influence the higher-ups, you will be without the resources to perform your job.

If the company allows you to talk to the person who used to do your job, you can ask him or her questions regarding the willingness of the higher-ups to respond to your suggestions.

If you are getting hints from the incumbent that your supervisor and the senior management are implacable, beware. Any changes that you feel should be made in order to help you do your job better will be ignored or shelved.

You Must Have a Proper Staff

Regardless of your title and nominal authority, you will not be able to do your job without a competent and loyal staff. Key people who will help you do your job include secretaries, administrative assistants, and others who get you information, type your letters, and the like.

Of course, some jobs don't require an actual staff. You may be working at a computer terminal, you may be a researcher in an R & D department or an internal consultant. Even if the company is unwilling to give you the personal assistance you may desire, you should at least find out if they will provide you with a pool of labor that can help you do the job. Very often, in fields such as advertising, you have access to a common pool of secretaries, copywriters, and art designers. What you must determine before you finish your series of interviews is the availability of these "commonly owned" staff persons. If you have to wait in line for the one typist on staff, you may find your career at the company sabotaged. This is what happened to our friend Susan and her co-workers.

If you really want to know whether you will have support to do your job, try to meet your staff before you take the job. Try to get a read on the degree to which they will support your efforts. What are their competencies? And, can you replace them if you have to? According to Carol Aloisi, it is important for you to make sure that you have the staff needed to perform the job and can fill vacancies as they arise.

If the proper performance of your job requires a staff, you should know what the procedures are to hire the people you want and fire or replace the people that you think don't fit in with your overall game plan. You may have to have a full discussion with personnel about the steps involved in these processes.

Getting the Budget You Need

If you are put into a management, supervisory, or departmental leadership position, having money to spend becomes one of the most crucial components of adequate or superior job performance. Whether you need it to hire personnel, buy a new word processor, or print training manuals, the budget that you are given can make or break you in the new position.

A large budget signifies two things. First, of course, it allows you to do the job better. If you have the budget, you can hire staff, get the superior workers you require, and maybe even secure consultants who can train and assist your staff. But more than that, it demonstrates to you that the company is committed to helping you succeed. This is as much a demonstration of company support as a large salary. Management is also signaling its trust that you will exercise good judgment in spending this money, whether on new personnel or new equipment.

If the company seems to be resisting giving you the big budget, you must sell them on what you will give them back in exchange for the funds. Stipulate why you need the money and insist that without this budget you cannot possibly accomplish the goals you and they agree you must achieve.

I should mention that departmental budgets can affect your ability to do the job regardless of your position. Even if you are the departmental typist, the total budget can affect your raises, your total work load, and even the quality of your typewriter.

Access to Resources

How important to your career is access to organizational resources? In Susan's case her inability to get near a computer became one of the many factors preventing her from doing her job. You must be able to use all the resources, be they conference rooms, company transportation, copying machines, data bases, or computers.

You must also know whether your staff will have the resources to do its job. One of my respondents had been promised at her interview that her secretary would be given a word processor. She didn't find out until she had assumed the position that the machine given her secretary was a first-generation relic. She never thought to ask at the interview exactly what kind of equipment the secretary would be using. It took six months to rectify this situation, a period in which the secretary plodded along with a piece of inferior office technology.

Don't ever assume that you will enjoy access to re-sources. Find out beforehand what the company offers (or is willing to purchase for you) in terms of equipment. As most of my interviews have confirmed, you are in a better position to lobby for resources before you take the job than after.

You Can't Do Your Job Without Information

Access to information is crucial in determining whether you can do the job. You must know whether the information you need to do your job will be at your fingertips and if information is being passed on to you accurately. There are several ways to get information—through computers, the grapevine, colleagues, and internal memos. If you are a sales or product manager, information is crucial. Ask at the interview how you get the information you need to do your job.

According to Walter Sonyi of Goodrich and Sherwood, part of being able to do a job is knowing whom to pester for information. It is important to know that you can go to a higher-up for the information you need. Making the right move depends on your own ability and willingness to indulge in pestering and the willingness of those above you to spend some time filling in the gaps in your knowledge. Without information, you will always underachieve.

At one consulting company I researched, consultants are encouraged to request information from their managers to ensure quality service to their clients. Since the consultant spends more time with the client than at home base, it is important that he or she be able to forward any questions about policy and procedure immediately to the central office. This prevents misunderstandings in the relationship with the client.

According to one respondent, at the time of the interview with the prospective company you can't always get a feeling whether senior management will be open to being questioned on policy and practices. Many bosses, she says, appear more unapproachable than they later turn out to be:

> I've worked for a variety of bosses. I've had bosses that basically never wanted to see anyone. But they always saw me. I'd find out what their routine was. If they were in early, I'd be at their door at 7:30. I would present my ideas then.

You can ask directly if people will be on hand to answer questions. Since your job performance depends directly on your access to a knowledge base, you want assurances that you and your staff will receive the information needed to do the assigned job.

Withstanding Pressure

A good part of your job performance may depend on your ability to stand up under pressure. People often fail not because of any lack of skills, power, or resources but because they are unable to endure the brutal pace of the job.

Some people thrive on pressure. They love to know that they have only twenty-four hours to complete a report or must travel all over the country on a moment's notice. Some work best knowing that if they don't complete their work, a big deal will fall through or a major loan will be aborted.

Other people realize that they can only work under broad mandates to perform a job over a long period of time. They cannot stand the pressure to complete a project with a tight deadline.

Which kind of person are you? How do you react to pressure, deadlines, tight time frames? One of the respondents for this book tells what it is like working at the Neilsen organization. Neilsen is one of the major suppliers to television and radio networks and advertisers of the infamous ratings—the reports of how many people watched "Dallas," "Dynasty," "Hollywood Bloopers," and the Superbowl. You would be astounded at the detail of these reports: They reveal not only the number of people who watched a particular program but a breakdown by age, sex, income, and so on.

The most amazing feature of these reports is not merely their detail but the fact that they are often constructed within only twenty-four to forty-eight hours. And the account executive, the one in charge, does not merely oversee the production of the reports but must make a full presentation of the findings to the client.

It is not uncommon for people to quit under the pressure and frustration certain pressurized positions involve. Lately we have been hearing much about the fortunes made by young people working as investment bankers for such companies as Salomon Brothers and Goldman Sachs. But imagine, if you will, staying calm while a manager of a pension fund wants you to find a repository for millions of dollars within the next twenty minutes. You have a short time to make a decision affecting the savings of millions of workers, and a bad decision could hurt your firm and possibly your career!

You must find out about the job's pressures to know if you are making the right move. Ask the interviewers whether deadlines are intrinsic to the job or if you work under broad mandates. If the job in question is located in a large firm's R & D department, you may never be expected to produce a useful "applied" product. But in an advertising company you may have to change an ad on the spot. And some marketing firms are known to have periods in which the core staff works twenty-four hours straight under ruthless pressure.

You will have to assess whether you are involved in the company's long-term projects or their life-and-death programs. The pressure is heaviest in the sectors of the company that involve production, delivery, and distribution.

Many people can stand the pressure as long as it is equally shared with coworkers. Unfortunately, it is an idiosyncrasy of many organizations that some people do the bulk of the work. This in itself can lead to a pressurized situation. One respondent at a major research firm relates how her manager will take on any project that the top people propose. Because this manager assumes that the staff can complete any project thrown at it, the work load is unbearable. Seven-day workweeks are not unheard of. The woman had no idea at the time she took the position that the work load would be so heavy. What makes her situation particularly grating is that most employees of the company work nine to five, Monday through Friday.

A last determinant of your ability to deal with pressure is your overall health. There are some people who, for health reasons, would be physically unable to do a job. You must be totally honest with yourself on the health issue, or failure to perform your job would be the least of your worries after six months performing in a pressurized environment.

Your ability to do the job is based on a combination of factors. Your skills, and the willingness of the company to help you improve them, are one set of factors. But you must also be cognizant of the organizational factors that can sabotage your ability to do the job. Consider these factors when you are thinking of taking a position in a given company.

I would like to mention one last word to those of you, like college students and homemakers, who are just entering the work force. You, more than others, probably have reason to be concerned about your ability to perform your prospective job, mainly because of your limited full-time work experience. Almost any position that you choose will by definition be an entry-level, learning position. You above all others should be particularly concerned about the available training.

However, if you are just about to enter the work force, there is one demographic factor in your favor. The coming labor shortage is inducing companies to become increasingly involved in training new workers. They assume that they cannot draw on a large pool of workers with great experience in the company's particular field, industry, or skill area. Companies are more than ever prepared and even eager to provide on-the-job or more formal training to the new worker. For many companies, this may be the only way to ensure the future availability of a skilled work force.

Only when you are sure you can do the job do you know if you are making the right move.

CHAPTER 6

♦ ♦

What You Must Know About Company Politics

You would be surprised at the extent to which an organization's politics can affect whether you actually succeed or fail in a job. A company's poor political climate can slow down or destroy the career of an up-and-coming manager. It also can make the job experience particularly unpleasant. A while back, when you evaluated your present company, you based part of your decision to leave or not to leave on the political climate of your current organization. In this chapter we will examine the kinds of questions that you should be asking about your prospective company's political climate before signing on. We will be especially concerned about identifying which types of situations should be avoided altogether.

There are several factors related to company politics that you must take into account if you want to ensure that you are making the right move. First, you must be able to pick up on the subtle indicators of corporate politics and judge whether the environment of your prospective company is going to harm or help your career. Second, you ought to evaluate whether you are a good political gamesman. Office politics can be a boon or bane, depending both on the severity and viciousness of the other players and your own ability to play the game. Third, you must know if the company itself has developed ways to deal with employee conflict.

The point is that you don't want any surprises when you join the company. You want to be as sure as possible that you are not moving into a political situation you are unable to handle.

Picking Up on Political Situations

You can ask the company about benefits, perks, what you will do day to day on the job, and promotional policies. In fact, you can inquire into just about any issue that this book covers. The only thing you can't ask about directly is the political situation. You want to know about the existence of factions, how your peers will accept you, and a number of other issues. Unfortunately, you will have to gather much of this information unobtrusively, from innuendo and suggestion.

YOUR BOSS AND THE POLITICAL ENVIRONMENT

Throughout the book we've touched on the effect your boss or supervisor can have on your career, especially in such areas as your ability to do the job and gain access to resources. He or she is equally important in shaping the political environment in which you work. Here are a few things you should know about your supervisor in this regard.

◗ Is Your Boss in Political Hot Water?

Working for someone who is having political problems with peers and colleagues is one of the easiest ways of getting dragged into a corporate power struggle. Numerous respondents recounted how taking a position under a boss who had made enemies or was fighting political battles eventually led to them feeling some of the heat.

There is no sure way of avoiding this situation. You can try to get a feeling at the interview whether the boss is stepping on other people's toes. Sometimes your prospective boss will unconsciously offer insights into his or her potential for problems with little prompting on your part. The real egotist can't help displaying a need for power, even during an interview. In fact, many use these interviews to flaunt their real or imagined power by telling you how much of the organization they control or influence. Beware of this type of person. If a boss's bragging and general presentation of self is grating on your nerves after only an hour, you can imagine how he or she is perceived by fellow employees who have been putting up with it for years.

One executive claims that your prospective boss can give off certain subtle signs during the interview that indicate that he or she tends to abuse power and must constantly demonstrate control. For instance, most people can have their phone calls screened by secretaries and colleagues when necessary. They know that the interview should be interrupted only in an emergency. If the person sitting across from you seems to be inundated with phone calls during your hour together, this could mean one of two things. It could just be that the work load is so overwhelming that all calls require immediate response. Or it could signify that the manager is purposely letting those calls come through.

According to some observers, a person who takes calls during an interview is going out of his way to tell you how important he is, how the organization cannot exist for even an hour without his input. A person who needs to flaunt power so flagrantly has the potential to alienate colleagues and get into political hot water.

▶ Can Your Boss Run Political Interference for You?

We all run into political problems at times. We may accidentally offend a powerful senior manager, encroach on another person's territory, or get someone jealous because of our success. Regardless of the source of your problems, you want to know that you have a boss who has the ability and the willingness to help you out when you get in trouble. A mentor would ordinarily run interference for his protégé. But even if your boss doesn't become your mentor, you want to know your boss will protect you.

I knew of one young social worker at a private hospital who customarily came into work ten to fifteen minutes late. His immediate supervisor, a department head, tolerated his tardiness, because he felt that the quality of work and long hours the employee put into the job more than made up for this one weakness. The social worker's long commute was a sufficient excuse for his lateness, and besides, the other workers didn't resent the supervisor's leniency.

A new hospital administrator was brought in to tighten things up and make the operation more cost effective. He thought that one of the areas he should attack first was the number of hours workers put in. He began to check closely the length of the workers' lunch hours and the time they came and went. He noticed this young person's arrival time and decided to make an example of him. Without so much as discussing the issue with the employee or the department head, the administrator put the young worker on nine-months' probation, informing him that for this period his comings and goings would be watched and clocked, and unless he shaped up he would be "shipped out."

The department head quickly recognized that this was not only an intolerable breach of authority but a political situation from which the social worker would have to be protected. The action showed disrespect for the worker and the department. Without hesitation the supervisor ran off a memo to the administrator stating that unless the probation was immediately rescinded he would order his whole department to walk off the job. The shocked administrator caved in.

Before you take a job, you want to know that you will have strong support from above. While you don't want any special favors, you do want to know that you will be protected from forces beyond your control.

Remember, regardless of how good a corporate swimmer you are, you can be sucked under by choppy political waters.

How do you know whether your boss will give you political protection? You can sometimes use the boss's reputation as a key. You may have heard of his or her political habits. But you will most likely have to rely on the cues emitted during the interview. In what way does the boss talk about subordinates—with apparent concern for what happens to them, or with a certain distance and indifference? You will have to be adept at picking up signals of attitude toward subordinates if you want to know whether this boss will expend energy getting you out of political trouble.

TWO BOSSES CAN MEAN DOUBLE TROUBLE

Beware of any job situation in which you are expected to report to two different division heads. Sometimes jobs are structured in such a way that you will report directly to one boss but have to give weekly or monthly statements to another. One gives the orders, but both have a varying amount of veto power over your actions.

Be careful in these situations. If the two are not getting along, you could find yourself in the middle of an interpersonal rivalry that could have bad effects on your career. You will have the opportunity to speak to both of them before you take the job. Make sure you clarify which one has the final say over your activities. Who does the evaluating? And who has the power to pull you off one project and put you on another?

YOU AND YOUR SUBORDINATES

Your supervisor can influence the political environment, but in many cases your subordinates are the ones who create it. If you are a manager, a good relationship with your staff is essential. Unfortunately, there are some conditions for which you are not responsible but that can affect your chances of success at the company.

You may think it impossible to know if your subordinates will support you before you take the job. After all, meeting them may not provide sufficient insight into their personalities to allow you to measure support. But there are some situations that should signal to you that you might be facing a problem if you take the job.

▶ Are You Just Another Supervisor?

The position you are filling may be a high-turnover position. That is, there may have been several managers who have tried out in this position and either didn't work out or were moved up quickly. This situation may make the subordinates view all incumbents as mere transients, tenants in a structure the staff actually owns and controls. They might feel that they, not you, really run the show. Many a secretary of state and director of the CIA have felt after a few months in the job that the tail was wagging the dog—that the lifetime civil servants supposedly under their command did just about what they wanted regardless of policy handed down from above.

You cannot read the hearts and minds of your subordinates. You cannot tell from a few preemployment discussions whether they will actually regard you as more than a transitory manager. But do find out from your superiors how many people have held this job and why they all left. Their responses should give you some insight into the situation.

Unless the company can give you a good reason why no one lasts in your prospective job, avoid a revolving-door position.

◗ Filling a Favorite's Shoes

Many companies have a policy of recruiting few if any outsiders. Employees work their way into higher positions by moving from the bottom up. Yet, under special circumstances these companies may obtain higher-level personnel from the outside if they cannot obtain the talent within the organization. Regardless of past tendencies to recruit from within, companies that are making a major transition to a new product line or changing policy direction must look for outside talent. Companies like AT&T are finding themselves in such predicaments.

You might have been offered this job because your experience fits the new mold. There is a good possibility, then, that you were given the job over a now-obsolete veteran worker. Since this person may have built up a strong relationship with his or her co-workers, who are now your colleagues, you may be heading for interpersonal difficulties.

You could easily end up resented by the entrenched staff. As an outsider, you may be stepping on toes and be denied much support from below. You may become part of a bad political environment.

You should definitely inquire about how the job came about. Has it been through a cutback? People may resent you because you have been hired while others were let go. What's important here is that they may also be demoralized. Only when you know the facts surrounding your hiring can you begin to deal with any subsequent political fallout.

◗ Supervising a Potential Rival

Sometimes you will not only be hired for a position that was to have gone to a company favorite, but you may be left with that person as your subordinate. This can be a very dangerous political situation. If this person has extensive influence with his or her peers, now also your subordinates, this influence can be used to challenge your authority.

I saw a horrendous example of this. One young man was brought into a company supposedly to run its marketing department. He was hired by the president of the company, who maintained a hands-off attitude toward the running of the company. The vice president of marketing, to whom the young man directly reported, wanted his protégé, a female administrative assistant, to get the job. The woman and the vice president literally ganged up on the newcomer at every turn, overruling his decisions and ignoring his suggestions. It got to the point where he felt that the VP and the administrative assistant were totally excluding him and making policy behind closed doors. After two years, realizing that he was not going to be able to overcome the political climate, he quit.

What is so unfortunate here is that he could have picked up on this situation before he took the job if he just had been sensitive to the clues being dropped all over the place. For instance, the vice president he ended up working for insisted that he be interviewed by the administrative assistant. It was an informal interview over lunch, but he still should have noticed how odd such a request was. It should have told him immediatley that something was out of kilter in the power structure. It was almost as though his "subordinate" were making the hiring decision.

Some executives suggest that people who find themselves in situations where they have to supervise potential rivals should not necessarily turn down the job. It is a problem that can be overcome by applying some common sense and using corporate diplomacy. For instance, you can try to transform an adversary into an ally. One respondent suggested that you confront or "caucus with" such a person right away, making it clear that you know he or she wanted the position and was probably qualified to get it. The idea to convey is, "If you play ball with me, I'll play ball with you. I don't intend to be here the rest of my life, and when I move up, I will either take you with me or recommend you for this job." You are letting your potential rival know that even though he or she didn't get the job, cooperation with you means upward movement in the organization on your coattails.

By doing this, you are offering the potential rival a stake in your own progress. Most good political gamesplayers understand that the best way to elicit cooperation from subordinates is to help them identify with you, to see your success as ultimately leading to their own. In the case of the potential rival, you are merely extending this principle.

If a conciliatory method fails, though, you may have to become confrontational. If someone is going behind your back, don't let it get out of control. Tell such a person "If you're not going to be on my team, then you have one option." He or she can resign.

This is another reason that you should most definitely find out before coming on board how much power you will have to hire and fire. Earlier we discussed your ability to get rid of incompetent staff. Here your concern is how to ditch potential troublemakers.

If these actions seem a brand of political hardball that you find particularly distasteful, then you shouldn't take a job in a company or department with a difficult climate. Only if you can play politics will you know that this type of situation is the right move.

◗ Are You Hired as a Potential Star?

Be careful if your supervisor bills you as a potential company superstar. Very often upper managers, who bolster their reputations by surrounding themselves with bright young comers, like to brag about how these young managers are quickly going to rise to the top. If you are one of the people brought in by this type of manager, realize that he may be creating a climate in which you will be deeply resented by subordinates and peers.

One person I interviewed came into a big sales position as a total novice. His champion knew of his reputation in other fields and felt that he could make a smooth transition into sales and, later, marketing. The president was going around telling people that he would "knock the socks off" everybody at the company. Many of his colleagues thought he couldn't do the job and would probably bring down the overall sales figures of the department. Account managers, who should have played an integral role in his learning experience, would not cooperate.

Again, the outcomes of situations such as these depend to a great part on your willingness and ability to play politics. He knew that he would have to prove himself to all involved because of the burden put on him by an effusive boss. But after his first big selling quarter, he won the respect of his colleagues. One of the account managers who had originally been most resentful even gave him an encouraging call. After all, he wanted to be on the good side of this budding superstar.

COMPANY COALITIONS: BANE OR BOON?

In a perfect world, employees of all organizations would keep their nose to the grindstone, work hard, and try to increase their productivity. Unfortunately, in a world where power, status, and salaries are distributed unequally, people let jealousy and greed influence their actions. Factions develop in organizations because people feel that alliances will help them get a share of power and other rewards that they might not secure on their own. These factions can make life hell for the organizational newcomer.

Very often, there is hostile competition within the company that may limit your future there. It could, for instance, hamper your movement within the company from one division to another. Interdivisional rivalry could be so great that any time you attempted to move to another part of the company your current peers and superiors would consider you disloyal.

You will be fortunate if you can get inside information on a company's bad politics. Word about such situations can spread quite quickly through professional organizations and the business world in general. The press can be merciless in divulging news of political rivalries within key businesses.

Some of my respondents have come up with quite ingenious ways to detect the existence of negative coalitions in a prospective company. If you undergo a round-robin type of interview, pay close attention to what the managers are saying about each other. Veterans of academic interviews become masters at assessing the political environment through these multiple interviews. Young candidates for a professional position undergo a series of interviews with chairmen, deans, and faculty members. By keeping their ears open they will hear the subtle comments faculty make about the chairman and the innuendos dropped by the college president about the department.

Being observant can help you avoid a dangerous political situation and make the right move.

◗ Don't Become a Pawn

You should try to assess not only if factions exist but if you will be expected to take sides. I have witnessed several of these political arrangements that negatively affected young employees. One of my respondents had been an up-and-coming financial analyst for a major accounting firm. He found himself embroiled in a battle between two factions that were trying to take over the firm. Each was attempting to load up its side with new partners to form a voting majority. He was mentored by one of the principals, who was attempting to raise him to partner. The resentment of those in the other faction made his life there quite unbearable.

While it is sometimes beneficial to be a member of a faction, you want to know before taking a job that there isn't bitterness between groups. Many a young academic has become embroiled in bitter rivalries between departmental factions and been unable to get the necessary votes for tenure. This denial of tenure has nothing to do with publications or teaching talent. It is based on the fact that an opposing faction refuses to provide the necessary votes.

◗ Nepotism

The strongest type of company faction, and the one into which you will have the least chance of gaining membership, is the one composed of the company owner's family. You will quickly find out that the family members make the major decisions and obtain the key corporate positions. The existence of this faction is not something you will suddenly learn of the day you start the job. During your interviews you will meet the founder, his or her sons and daughters, and various other relatives—all employees and officers of the company. For better or worse, this political faction will control decisions and will probably occupy the best positions.

Recently there was a furor in the press over the fact that the Ruder & Finn public relations company employs so many members of the family. The media focused on the fact that talented nonfamily employees, disgusted that family members ran the show, were leaving in droves. Most of these employees felt that they had no real future in the company, since the good jobs were held by relatives of one of the owners. Even clients of the company were expressing dissatisfaction with this flagrant nepotism, claiming that it was affecting the quality of the company's service.

If you are considering entering a family-run business, realize that its unique politics can severely limit your career there. Unless you become a family favorite, you will never get to the top spots. I know many managers who have become quite frustrated being constantly overriden by the clan members who exercise final say over company policy. You may even have to take orders from younger family members put in key positions by a founder who thinks it would be nice if they had some experience running a department or division. Personnel decisions in a family-run concern can be capricious and unfair.

IS THE COMPANY IN REBELLION?

Sometimes top management hands down policy decisions that imply great change for the company. It could be a decision to reorganize the corporation, initiate a new product or market campaign, or restructure the compensation structure. Any of these changes can realign the reporting structure, encroach on some employee's customary power, and generate backbiting and infighting.

In Susan's case from Chapter Five, her company had made a basic decision to change its direction from one of selling only insurance to offering a complex array of financial services and products. She entered the company during this time of transition and in fact was hired to be part of this new direction. But there was great resistance from members of the middle echelons of the particular division she joined. They never really accepted this policy change and were uncooperative in the training and preparation that the new recruits needed to be successful on the job. Susan was caught in the middle of a political situation over which she had no control.

You shouldn't have to dig deeply to discover if a company is undergoing changes in direction. The company will probably inform you of the change during your interviews.

Some job hunters are undaunted by this situation, and in fact see it as a growth opportunity they can take

*advantage of. Only you can tell if your political acumen
makes going with such a company the right move.*

Are You a Political Animal?

Your ability to weather company politics should be an
important part of the decision to take a job. What is a
dangerous political environment for some is manage-
able for others. In the world of organizational politics,
one person's meat is almost certainly another person's
poison.

So, once you have assessed the political environment, you must then determine your abilities in the
political ring. Can you play the game? Assess your
own abilities closely before you automatically reject a
position that has political overtones.

Many executives and others claim that politics is a
fact of life, something that cannot be avoided. They
think that you should learn how to play the game and
manage yourself in the political environment.

Some people are good at playing politics and use
factions and infighting to their own advantage. Look at
your past experience in organizations. Are you good at
striking compromises with opponents? Do you know
how to placate potential rivals? Can you form alliances
with potential friends? And do you have experience
playing politics?

Before you can play politics successfully, you have
to be able to recognize if factions exist, who belongs to
each, and what the competing parties want. I firmly
believe that in playing organizational politics you are
halfway there if you can first correctly analyze the situ-

ation. Some people are just better than others in analyzing the dynamics of power situations. They have an uncanny sense of factional alignments.

Very often the best corporate politicians are those who can stay friendly with all factions without joining any. Although this is the most difficult position to maintain, it may be the best. Do not become emotionally attached to any particular faction. While it is not easy to avoid falling into the "we-them" mind-set, those who can keep their minds clear of emotional allegiances will maintain the necessary objectivity to survive. These people put their own objectives first and join alliances because they serve their purposes, not to fulfill a personal need to feel part of a group.

Beyond your ability to make alliances or correctly perceive the alignment of factions, there is one important factor in navigating choppy political waters. It is the extent to which you have the stomach to play political hardball. Many people just don't have it in them to persistently confront subordinates, play both sides of the fence, and expend the sheer energy it takes to make it in some corporate political environments. You should ask yourself some hard questions about your willingness to fight the good fight before descending into the political cauldron.

Does the Company Have a Way to Deal with Conflicts?

Sometimes organizations solve political problems by either preempting conflict before it occurs or appeasing the already feuding parties.

IBM is one company that has become expert in diffusing conflict and developing cooperation. When subordinates have conflicts with supervisors, they can utilize a so-called skip-level interview to pass over a couple of organizational levels to discuss a grievance with upper management. Top executives usually move quickly to resolve conflict. At this giant corporation, if supervisors abuse their power over subordinates, they are assigned to what has become known as the "penalty box." The offending superiors are given lower level jobs at a less desirable location or department, where they can "ponder their mistakes."

If a company has formal means of settling disputes and engages those methods often, you can probably rest a little easier knowing that politics will have minimal effects on your career at this organization. By institutionalizing conflict resolution, the company decreases the possibility of politics getting out of hand.

One sign that a company has an interest in keeping the lid on political problems is the regular training of supervisors to manage and resolve conflict. Some companies go to elaborate lengths to make sure that their people are trained in the art of negotiation. Ask the interviewers if these kinds of training programs exist. The courses might have titles like "managing conflicts" or "how to handle your workers" and might be given on site or at a training institute. If your prospective company is regularly engaged in such training, you can be confident that it understands the reality of company politics and is ready to tackle the problem head-on.

You should also inquire whether the company regularly brings in outsiders to deal with political problems. Mediation is a growing and changing field. At one time mediators or arbitrators were strictly involved with labor negotiations and union-management discussions.

But increasingly corporations are turning to specialists in "organizational development" to help groups handle conflict. These outside consultants adopt a variety of methods to lessen the effects of organizational politics. They sit with conflicting parties and get them to talk to each other, teach managers how to handle recalcitrant subordinates, and engage in managed confrontation to prevent uncontrolled infighting.

Very often these discussions are not limited to conflict situations. Senior management may realize that to prevent conflict it has to establish an atmosphere of cooperation. So the outside consultants are brought in not to just mend fences but to establish permanent working arrangements between various members of a work group, department, or whole organization.

There is nothing worse than seeing a newcomer to an organization, one who has little stake in company politics and who is totally blameless, get sucked into the vortex of office politics. Truth be told, you would be better off avoiding some jobs that have bad political environments. The pettiness and backbiting can force out even the best gamesplayer.

All companies have political situations. There are just some that are horrendous and should be avoided. You have to be able to assess both the political environment and your ability to survive in it if you want to make the right move. And you must also feel that the organization has a handle on its own internal dynamics and is committed to dealing with interpersonal problems and interfactional conflicts as they arise.

CHAPTER 7

♦♦♦♦♦♦♦♦♦♦♦♦♦♦♦♦♦♦♦♦♦♦♦♦♦♦

The Job and Your Life

There is more to a job than its pay, promotional possibilities, and politics. You must also be concerned about the relationship between the prospective job and your personal life. A company or job can impact on your life in two major ways. First, a company can make your life easier by intervening in critical areas of your life. The employer, for instance, can ease relocation or assist in such matters as maternity leave and child care. Second, a company can provide personal services that you may not ordinarily have access to, such as nutritional programs, stress management, and so on.

The extent to which a company impacts on your personal life can ultimately determine whether joining an organization is the right move.

This chapter will deal with the variety of such issues you must keep in mind when evaluating the next job.

When Taking the Job Means You Have to Move

Perhaps the greatest impact a job can have on your life-style is when the company expects you to relocate. The problem may present itself immediately: The company may require you to uproot yourself to take the position. Or the relocation problem may be something you will face down the road. Perhaps you cannot get major promotions without relocating.

Relocations are by no means uncommon. According to Merrill Lynch Relocation Management, Inc., a major relocation firm, between 1983 and 1984 transfers in Fortune 1000 companies increased by 34 percent. In his or her lifetime, the average executive can expect to relocate four times. An Allied Van Lines study of CEOs showed that 76 percent had moved at least once during their careers; 20 percent had moved five or more times.

What makes these people so willing to uproot their families, change their life-styles completely, leave close friends, and face strange surroundings? The answers usually are money, promotion, increased status, and position. For many executives, geographic relocation is the only route to the top.

Does your prospective company want you to relocate? If so, as you ponder moving halfway across the country to gain a 50 percent increase in salary, you will have to measure these newfound riches against the effect of this relocation on the rest of your life. Here are some issues that should help you in your decision to go with this company.

IS IT THE NORMAL WAY OF MOVING UP?

The first thing you must know about a company before you sign on is whether you must regularly relocate in order to get ahead. Some companies, like IBM, consider regular movement of their managers part of their education and corporate training. If you don't see the countrywide operation of IBM, you are not considered properly trained. Of course, this philosophy tells you right away to expect relocation as a basic fact of life. Refusing to move can quickly take you off the fast track.

If the company tells you that you can only acquire the skills and experience they consider important at their corporate headquarters in another state, realize that relocation is a basic requirement for upward mobility there.

While most companies will not spring relocation on you, some have been known to ask new employees to move unexpectedly. So make the company clarify its requirements regarding the relocation. If there are circumstances that would inhibit your movement around the country or the world, say so. Camouflaging your life-style limitations at the interview just to get a job will only lead to misunderstandings later on.

WILL THEY FIND A JOB FOR YOUR SPOUSE?

Even if you are willing to relocate, there are numerous other issues you should question the company about. One is the impact of the move on your spouse's career.

Companies increasingly have to deal with the fact that their employees' spouses work. Because of this change in the family relationship, companies cannot just move their employees without helping the spouses find a new job. Couples and headhunters I interviewed for the book expressed the belief that companies are now ready more than ever to help the so-called trailing spouse find a job at the new locale.

There are several options that companies provide to the coveted employee. They can go as far as hiring an employment counselor or executive headhunter for your mate. Wang Laboratories circulates the trailing spouse's résumé and makes company facilities available to help in the job search. Sometimes, in order to secure the person they are recruiting, Wang even hires the spouse.

These packages get quite elaborate. Besides hiring an employment specialist to help the trailing spouse get a résumé together and review employment possibilities, one company also tried to line up prospective interviews in key companies and introduce the spouse to community leaders who might be able to influence the person's career. In short, the company utilized its own influence within the economic community to land the spouse a job.

In making your decision to go with a company, you must evaluate how much the loss of your spouse's income will affect your standard of living. You must assess how much help your spouse would need in finding a new job. Be as up front as possible with your prospective company about your spouse's job needs. And don't hesitate to bargain!

WHAT THE COMPANY CAN OFFER TO EASE YOUR RELOCATION

There is an enormous array of financial packages that companies put together these days to lure the best and the brightest. Relocation can be traumatic enough emotionally without an added financial burden. So, during your interviews, you should find out from the personnel officer just what the company can do for you financially to ease your move.

◗ House-hunting Costs

If you do take a job in a new location, you will probably need to acquire a house or apartment before you actually start working. Hence, you may have to make several trips to your new site in order to visit realtors, become familiar with relative housing costs, and view all prospective houses. Many companies now cover all expenses associated with hunting for a house, including airfares, rental cars, hotels, meals, and entertainment. Companies will often pay for at least three trips, some even assuming your baby-sitter expenses while you make the trips to look for the house.

◗ Temporary Living Costs

Sometimes even several house-hunting trips are not sufficient to make a good housing decision. Thus, when evaluating a prospective company, you want to know whether it will pay your temporary living costs. You and your family may have to live in a motel or hotel for several weeks while you continue to look for a house or condo. The company should also pay for storage of your household furniture during this period, and since you probably can't cook in this environment, your new employer should also pay at least some of your restaurant bills.

Of course, the dollar amount is negotiable. But you should try to ascertain whether your prospective employer has a policy of paying for any temporary living expenses. Then you can bargain for what you think you will need if you cannot find housing immediately.

♦ Direct Moving Costs

Moving yourself and your family can run into thousands, and the company's policy on assuming moving costs may well be a deciding factor in whether you can afford to take the job. Many people take positions without finding out whether the company will absorb this expense.

You should clarify whether the company is picking up the bill for the move, including such hidden costs as transportation for the family and pets and mileage allowances for the movement of your automobile.

Remember, it is often too late to find out about these services after you accept the job.

♦ Mortgage Differentials

One of the more distressing aspects of relocating is the discovery that the new house must be purchased at a mortgage rate several points higher than you are currently paying. This new mortgage can quickly eat into your new job's higher salary. If you suddenly find yourself confronting a substantially higher mortgage rate, you should definitely find out if your prospective employer will agree to make up the dollar difference between the old mortgage rate and the new, higher rate, at least for the first four or five years of your employment. Increasingly, companies are agreeing to such arrangements.

♦ Expenses-paid Return Trips

Even after you relocate, there will probably be several aspects of your old life that will require continued attention. You may have to still pick up mail, pack-ages, and deliveries at the old address. You may have uncompleted business in the old town. Or you may just be finishing up work at the family dentist. In any event, you will want to know whether the prospective employer will provide expenses-paid return trips to your former locale. You should discuss the amount, frequency, and duration of these trips during your job interview.

THE QUALITY OF LIFE OF THE NEW LOCATION

You will be spending thirty-five to fifty hours per week at the job. The rest of the time, you will be living in a community. And the quality of your life outside the job will be a major factor determining whether taking the job is the right move.

The simplest way to evaluate the attractiveness of your prospective employer's community environment is to ask yourself what you like and dislike about the area you are currently living in. Through this process you can straighten out in your own mind whether you would be happy in the new location.

There are several factors you should consider. For instance, will you be living in a city, suburb, small town, or rural area? For many people accustomed to a large city, the transition to a small town is unbearable. The absence of museums, theater, and movies could drive a city person to distraction. No one was surprised when few employees of the New York office of Ameri-can Express Company agreed to accompany the or-ganization in its recent move to Utah. It wasn't the distance that discouraged the workers; it was the cul-tural mismatch between the two areas.

If you have kids, you have to be concerned about the quality of the public school system. If your prospective employer is located in a city with a run-down school system, you may be forced to send your kids to an expensive private school.

Access to shopping is something that should also be considered. If your new locale is a small town, you will not have access to the many stores and huge malls common to large cities and suburbs. Will you have access to a large city?

And what choice of neighborhoods, and hence neighbors, will you have? Will you be the only executive in a blue-collar area or the only businessperson in an academic community?

RELOCATION IS A FAMILY DECISION

In a study of dual-career couples, researchers found that three-fourths of the women who followed their husbands had substantial negative reactions to the move. Couples recounted horror stories about how the move hurt their marriage.

Relocation is not a simple process. Your wife or husband might have to find a new job. And if the spouse doesn't work, he or she will be left to deal on an everyday basis with an unfamiliar community, neighbors, and repairmen. The impact on your kids could be especially traumatic. The kids will be leaving their schools, friends, and familiar surroundings—in short, a good portion of their emotional support network. It may be very hard for you to justify relocation to your kids in terms of your career goals. All they know is that some important components of their lives will be gone forever.

We should not be surprised at the relocation experts' reports that, on average, families take a full two years to settle in after a relocation, if they settle in at all. Moving is considered a stress-producer equal to divorce or the death of a loved one.

Because of the gravity of relocation, you must make this particular decision a family one. You must discuss the prospective move as openly as possible with your spouse and kids. Point out why you want the new job, and get them to open up about their objections to and majors fears about the relocation. Whenever possible, it is advisable to take the whole family on a visit to the new area to get a feeling for what their responses will be if you all do move there.

The right move involves more than finding the right job at a good salary. The job will quickly mean nothing if your family is unhappy with their new life, a life made necessary by your career needs. Their later resentment, regardless of how subtly they express it, can turn an otherwise good career experience sour.

GETTING THE INFORMATION YOU NEED ABOUT YOUR NEW LOCALE

If the company you are considering is located in an area about which you have little or no information, there are several things you can do to find out more.

Very often, companies will provide an all-expenses-paid exploratory trip to your prospective location. If they really want you, they will consider it a good investment to let the new area sell itself.

A simple way to assess your prospective area is the *Rand McNally Places Rated Almanac*. This volume, which is updated regularly, contains in-depth discussions of a wide variety of locations and also numerically rates such factors as "ambiance."

One of your big concerns will be the cost of living of the new city you are considering and how far your new salary will go in this environment. The best way to get this information, of course, is to have the prospective company's personnel officer provide pertinent price data. In the unlikely event that these data aren't available, the company can commission a comparative cost-of-living analysis on the new city. You will want information on such things as home values, income taxes, homeowners' insurance, the cost of schooling, real estate taxes, and so on. The company might enlist the services of a management consulting firm experienced in such information-gathering.

Remember that the more your company is willing to do to ease your relocation, the more you can be sure they are interested in acquiring you as an employee. Their activity in this regard is more than a service; it is a show of faith. However, if the company is unwilling or unable to provide such information, you can do your own research. A good place to start is the *Intercity Cost of Living Index*, published quarterly by the American Chamber of Commerce Research Association. This invaluable compendium lists 228 cities and compares the prices of a variety of goods and services, such as housing, utilities, transportation, and health care. It is available from the Louisville Chamber of Commerce, 1 Riverfront Plaza, Louisville, KY 40202. This volume and the Rand McNally guide should form the basis of a good solid search of an area.

Don't underestimate the advice of friends and family in regard to the quality of life of a prospective city or area. If the relocation director or personnel chief is telling you that "Minneapolis isn't bothered by snow" or "People in Orlando don't let the heat and humidity bother them," double-check these statements with friends and relatives living in these areas. Sometimes only "eyewitness informants" can give you the real insights into the annoying little characteristics that so many places reveal only after they are lived in for a while.

Not only do family and friends provide information, they also provide invaluable social contacts you can use if you do decide to accept the job. Inheriting a preestablished network of contacts who can show you the ropes can certainly ease settling in.

One final source of information is a relocation kit entitled *No False Moves* published by Catalyst, a career research organization. The kit consists of two cassettes and a corresponding workbook with exercises that will help you physically get the move going, possibly solve family dilemmas, and even negotiate many of the benefits we discussed.

Of course, this is only a partial compilation of all the issues involved in relocation. You will probably discover aspects of a given location that will be overwhelmingly attractive. However, your place of residence may be secondary to the promotion and pay increases awaiting you at the new job. As I point out throughout the book, your decision should be based on what you value most in life and in your job.

The Quality of Child Care—A Critical Factor

With over 50 percent of the adult female population currently in the work force, and with an ever-increasing proportion of women with children under six going to work, it is no surprise that the issue of child care is becoming critical in people's work lives. And it will probably be a factor in determining whether accepting a job is the right move.

Child care will be a factor if you are in any of the following conditions: you are a father whose wife works either full time or part time; you are an employed mother whose husband also works; you are unmarried with a child; or you plan at some time in the future to have children.

Companies are increasingly becoming involved in the care of their employees' children, but the particular type of involvement varies greatly. Occasionally, you will read an article that claims that "2000 companies now support day care for employees" or that headlines, "Employee Day Care on the Rise." And the company you are considering may indeed claim that it supports employee day care. But as we shall see, you will not be making the right move unless you know exactly what the interviewers mean by "supporting child care." Here's a look at the types of programs out there.

EMPLOYEE VOUCHER REIMBURSEMENTS

You should find out from personnel whether the company will reimburse you for costs that you incur at a private, family, or community day-care center.

Child care does not come cheap. The weekly fee at a community-run-day-care center can run as high as $100. The family day-care center, which usually involves a neighborhood woman watching a handful of local children, can cost about $50 per week per child. And you can expect to pay a trained live-in sitter $200 to $250 per week and $150 and up for one without formal training.

The employer voucher reimbursement program is designed to offset all or part of the employee's child care expenses. In this system the company either issues vouchers to the parents or pays the child care providers directly.

Ask personnel how you can become eligible for such a program. The mere existence of such a program does not guarantee your eligibility. Often the employer stipulates that the employee's spouse must be working or attending school in order for the family to receive this benefit. In other words, companies usually want some assurance that you really need this type of child care before they will reimburse you for such expenses.

While over 500 businesses, including Polaroid and the Ford Foundation, offer a variety of reimbursement programs, they are still a relatively rare offering. And these reimbursement programs vary greatly, with some companies offering total reimbursement, and others only partial.

INFORMATION AND REFERRAL (I & R) SERVICES

Again, let me make clear that a company's claim that it supports day care can mean any number of things. It may be offering nothing more than general information on child care and suggestions on how you can select high-quality service. The employer may also research local child care facilities and provide you with results of this research.

Over 900 companies offer information and referral services. For instance, IBM provides a large network of counselors and child care training programs. While this type of program is useful, it does little to defray the costs that you will incur if you and your spouse work and must find someone to take care of your child.

COMPANY OWNED AND OPERATED DAY-CARE FACILITIES

Many working parents hope that companies will establish and operate day-care facilities themselves. These facilities, usually located either on-site or near-site, cost less than many community-run centers. Sometimes this service is free. Approximately 225 companies, among them Hoffmann-LaRoche, Merck, Campbell Soup, Tandy, and Stride-Rite, operate their own day-care centers.

The benefits to you are obvious. Because the facility is on-site or near-site, you will be close enough to your children should anything go wrong. Because the center is owned and operated by your employer, you can feel more secure about the safety of your children (especially in light of the child-abuse incidents associated with many private day-care facilities). Also, you will have to do much less juggling of your work schedule. You can drop off and pick up your children on your way to and from work.

You should find out from your prospective company's personnel department whether there exists a waiting list for the program. You can imagine the demand for such a program. Most companies report that their on-site programs are working at full capacity. You should inquire into how long this waiting list is and when you can expect to enroll your children in this program.

You should ask to inspect the day-care facility. Does it have all of the services you think important, like a play area and good dining facilities? Does it seem safe? And what about the quality of the staff? Are there professional social workers on board?

INDIRECT SUPPORT OF EXISTING COMMUNITY PROGRAMS

Corporations are increasingly supporting already-existing community programs. Your prospective company may be providing space, services, or products for existing day-care programs, or it may be making charitable donations to such centers.

The receiving institution then reciprocates by giving the donating company's employees a tuition discount or priority admission. This type of support may be the wave of the future. The company can on the one hand make child care affordable to its employees and on the other hand avoid the problems associated with running its own day-care center.

Again, if this type of service is offered, examine closely what centers and programs are covered. You are not just concerned with cost. You must also look at the issue of quality.

SALARY-REDUCTION PROGRAMS

When your prospective employer talks about supporting child care, he or she may be referring to a salary-reduction program. In this type of program, your salary is decreased by the amount of your day-care expenses and the employer uses that money to pay the day-care provider. You save on taxes because your actual taxable salary is reduced. It is like being able to deduct from your income the entire cost of caring for your child. Unfortunately, these types of programs are coming under increased scrutiny by the IRS, and it is predicted that a severe cap will be placed on the amount you can deduct from your gross taxable income.

If you have the choice, opt for more direct assistance in the area of child care. Don't be afraid to make day care a bargaining issue. Companies are becoming increasingly cooperative in this area because they are seeing real results, such as higher productivity and lower turnover.

I would make one warning in regard to the effects of corporate day-care programs on internal company politics. Childless coworkers, who get no benefit at all from these programs, may feel that they are subsidizing out of their own pockets workers who decide to have children. This feeling may lead them to demand other financial compensation from the company.

Also, the fact that those employees utilizing on-site day-care facilities are permitted to leave their jobs at five o'clock to pick up their children, while the unmarried and childless instead have to pick up the slack in overtime, can lead to great resentment. The childless may feel that they are being shortchanged and somehow taken advantage of because they have no children.

Therefore, although we can categorically say that the availability of day care is a good reason to take a position in a company, realize that you may be required to assuage feelings of jealousy and resentment on the part of the childless regarding the day care "perk."

I should mention that most employers are still in the dark ages when it comes to providing adequate child care support programs. They often think it sufficient for the employee to take the federal child-care tax credit (in 1985 about $480 per child for those of middle income). Most studies claim that the tax credit absorbs only between 20 percent and 30 percent of your child support burden. But if your prospective employer has a good day-care support program, you ought to consider signing on with this company the right move.

The Job and Your Family Life

As we saw in the section on relocation, the job you choose can affect all family members. While making a geographic move has its obvious effects on the family, there are often subtle aspects of the job that can influence the quality of your personal life. The job may require you to spend time away from your family, or it may involve them in corporate life more than you or they would desire.

HOW MUCH TIME MUST YOU SPEND AWAY FROM THE FAMILY?

Your current job may have one advantage that you have taken for granted: It may afford you a lot of free time with your spouse and your children. Will you lose this free time in the new job? And how will this lack of free time affect your relationship with your family?

Many companies realize that working parents need time at home, so they provide flexible hours. Flexi-

time, as this program is popularly known, commonly
gives you the latitude to start work anywhere from
seven o'clock to nine o'clock in the morning and to
leave work between three and five. This type of plan
can allow you to coordinate your work time with your
personal life. Companies often require you to submit
your schedule ahead of time and will not allow changes
in this schedule without several weeks' notice. So you
can't suddenly decide on a Friday to come in later than
you usually do. Find out the specifics of this plan from
personnel.

   Travel is another feature of a job that can eat into
your time with your family. If your spouse works, and
you have children, it may be impossible to coordinate
your schedule with his or hers if the job requires heavy
travel. Responsibility for cooking, cleaning, and trans-
porting the kids may fall unevenly on the working
spouse when you are at a conference or sales meeting.
If travel is involved, discuss the job choice decision
thoroughly with your spouse.

YOUR FAMILY'S INVOLVEMENT IN COMPANY LIFE

You may like a company that seeks to involve your
family in the everyday camaraderie of the company.
Many corporations have family picnics and events that
boost employee morale and increase a sense of togetherness.

   But there is another type of involvement you may
not be able to live with easily. If you are a senior or
middle manager on the way up, you will from time to
time be expected to entertain clients and colleagues in
your home. Some companies are very candid about
this requirement. They may even interview family

members during the selection process in order to see if they project the "right image."

I have known job hunters to turn positions down because they sensed that their families would be intimately involved in meeting and entertaining clients in their homes. They couldn't live with the ruptured boundary between their jobs and their private lives.

If you are informed that your family may be expected to become involved in diverse aspects of corporate social life, you must discuss with your spouse and children their feelings about having to be on hand occasionally to mingle with colleagues and clients.

VACATIONS

If the job does require periods of time away from your family, sometimes a generous vacation plan and a liberal policy toward personal days can lessen the job's negative effects on your home life. Most companies start out their employees with two or three weeks' vacation, unless the job is in the civil service or the school system. But if you are leaving a job where you have already built up a longer vacation, you can make free time a bargaining issue.

The policy on personal days is important also. Some companies let you take an "unlimited" amount of personal days. While you don't want to abuse this privilege, it is good to know that if a family emergency comes up, you do have the freedom to take the day off to deal with it.

MATERNITY AND PATERNITY LEAVES

You must have the company clarify its policy in regard to time off to have and care for a baby. Companies vary widely on this issue. You want to know whether you will receive a paid or unpaid maternity leave. How much time after the birth of the child will you be able to stay out? How "protected" is your position while you're gone? Will they hire a temp, or anyone, for that matter, to do your job?

Companies are much more enlightened about maternity leaves than they are about giving the father time off to take care of the child. Many of the old sex-role stereotypes of the mother as prime actor in the birth process still prevail in corporate America. But the situation is changing even for fathers. Just make sure you understand the specifics of these policies.

The Company's Commitment to Your Personal Growth

The modern corporation is increasingly assuming many of the functions formerly performed by the family. The increased involvement of the corporation in providing day-care assistance is one example. But corporations are not stopping there. They are increasingly providing services to employees that enhance their sense of well-being and contribute to their personal growth.

When considering whether to take a position with a prospective employer, you may want to ask what type of program it offers in the area of personal growth. Though this particular type of program may not be a decisive factor in whether or not you accept a job offer, there is no doubt it could affect the quality of your work life and your life outside the job. Studies are already demonstrating a relationship between these programs and both a reduction in absenteeism and turnover and an increase in job satisfaction and productivity.

So, you should look carefully at what these companies are offering to improve the quality of your personal life.

HEALTH, NUTRITION, AND FITNESS

Companies are becoming increasingly enthusiastic about helping employees achieve physical fitness. And so they should, since studies show that healthy employees have better attendance records, are less of a drain on the health benefits program, and are more productive. With these advantages in mind, companies are embarking on a variety of personal health programs.

Johnson & Johnson, for instance, features what they label a "Live for Life" program, a comprehensive wellness program that offers information on and assistance with nutrition, stress management, weight control, and medical self-care. J & J even helps employees give up cigarettes. Union Carbide also has such a wellness program. The proven results of such programs include improved muscle tone, loss of body fat, a more optimistic outlook, improved sleep, increased energy, and decreased stress.

You should not take lightly the availability of such a program in your prospective company as a job choice factor. Any program which can help you work better should hasten your move up the corporate ladder. And, regardless of the effect such programs have on your promotional possibilities, they tend to make for a happier and more vibrant workplace.

Nutritional programs are also catching on. The municipal government of Birmingham, Alabama, has some 110 city workers participating in a nutritional program. People are losing weight and feeling better. And job satisfaction is increasing. Xerox includes a 350-calorie "heart saver" dish on each menu, plus a vegetarian plate. Many companies now enlist the consulting expertise of such organizations as Nutriwork, which offers ten-week seminars on nutrition-related diseases, food values, food labels, and methods of decreasing dietary fats and increasing fiber.

Again, you wouldn't take a job merely because the company offers such programs. But they may serve as an indication of the company's overall attitude toward its employees. This attitude may extend into other areas, such as a willingness to promote and grant raises. Obviously, companies with these programs care about the well-being of their employees.

STRESS MANAGEMENT

As mentioned in Chapter 5, your job performance can be affected by your ability to handle stress. While we are each ultimately responsible for handling our own stress, many companies now recognize that their employees may need help in meeting job pressures in order to become more productive.

These programs may take any number of forms. John Hancock Mutual Life Insurance Company, for instance, holds three-hour sessions that teach deep-muscle relaxation. Texas Instruments has a program that teaches relaxation, perception, and coping skills. Your prospective company may follow the lead of Adolph Coors and Co. and teach you how to deal with the stress of child rearing. Your company may even offer you incentives for participating in the stress-reduction plan.

You should keep in mind that if you are considering a job that offers a great deal of pressure along with its attractive pay and perks, you may want to know whether the company offers help in stress management. This may be a crucial factor in determining whether joining this company is the right move.

THE EMPLOYEE ASSISTANCE PROGRAM

These types of programs, known as EAPs for short, are aimed at helping the employee control and conquer such problems as drug and alcohol abuse. The term also encompasses personal and family therapy. Besides the obvious benefits of such programs, their existence also suggests that the company cares about the employees. Personnel will probably inform you of their existence without any prompting.

▶ Drug Testing and You

For better or worse, many companies are responding to the problem of employee drug use with measures more severe than EAPs. They feel the problem has gotten so bad they can't wait for employees to "fess up" and come in for help. They have resorted to mandatory drug testing.

The growth of drug testing at the workplace has led to a bitter controversy. Some companies are going so far as to screen all applicants with urinalyses. You may consider this as invasion of privacy or you may consider testing a necessary evil. Companies must inform you of their policy regarding testing.

You will have to make up your own mind about whether you want to work for a company that performs involuntary spot checks of its employees. Many consider drug use a private matter that is no concern of their employer. As of 1986, thirteen state legislatures had passed a variety of antitesting laws.

You should find out what the consequences of a positive drug test are. Will you be fired? Will the company retain you but insist that you attend rehabilitation? And how confidential is the test?

SABBATICALS AS A RELEASE

Some companies feel that giving their employees extended periods away from the office can help them become better workers. A growing number of companies are offering periodic sabbaticals to selected employees.

If you are in a particularly pressured environment, you may welcome such a hiatus. Like other programs, this particular one shows that the company cares about your personal life.

Long Hours

The number of hours you work will affect your life outside the job. Some jobs simply require that you sacrifice a substantial portion of your personal life and your leisure time to your job. There are people who think that the monetary and status rewards associated with these jobs make the sacrifice of a personal life worth it.

This issue was dealt with in a recent *Wall Street Journal* article on new business graduates' attitudes toward their "glamorous Wall Street jobs." The article referred to the jobs in the high-powered investment and law firms that promised big pay and high status. What many of the young people involved in these fields never anticipated were the hours involved in such a career. One woman who started at $50,000 a year at Morgan Stanley and Co. was fully prepared to work fifty to sixty hours a week in her area, analyzing takeover deals. But she often found herself working 90 to 100 hours a week. She eventually quit.

You should find out from the company exactly how many hours are involved in this business. Successful senior corporate executives spend about 58 hours a week at work. And in some investment banks and law firms, seven-day, 100-hour work weeks aren't uncommon. You may have to perform your job for long hours just to keep up.

No occupation is really safe from long hours. Even secretaries, who are usually thought of as inhabiting the standard nine-to-five world, can expect to pitch in with extra hours if the work load increases. You may be paid time and a half, but you won't be able to perform your household chores or go to the opera. And if you are a secretary to a rising star or already-established senior executive, you are truly subject to the vagaries of someone else's schedule. Many secretaries I speak with mention the occasional Sunday spent in the office.

Fields known for their sporadic and unpredictable schedules are market research, law, investment banking, sales, and consulting, to name a few. And in point of fact, if you are offered a so-called fast-track position in any field, you should expect that the job, not leisure, will become the major focus of your life.

You should decide early on just how much of your

personal life you are ready to sacrifice for a job. Long hours and the stress associated with this type of work can wreck your personal life. In the *Wall Street Journal* article, one thirty-five-year-old vice president of an investment company blames the unpredictability of his hours for a weakening of friendship bonds. His friends no longer accept his breaking appointments and dates.

The long hours required by some jobs seem to be especially frustrating to women. Time and again the women executives I interview claim to have a poor-to-nonexistent social life. Though most wouldn't give up the prestige and pay associated with their management jobs and skyrocketing careers, during interviews they openly admit that if they aren't willing to date fellow staff members, the chances of developing a relationship are quite low.

One young consultant, a woman in her early thirties, is giving a full six days each week to her job. This diligence has helped her become functional COO of the firm, but she admits that she sees few men. She recently joined a coed health spa and hopes that her social life will improve. But even if she meets someone, she will still have to give her job—with its long travel schedules and longer hours—priority over any nascent relationship. She is conscious of this situation and is willing to live with it for the sake of her career.

Interestingly, she mentioned that the only women who remain in the consulting field are those who don't get married and have kids. While some careers can coexist with family life, fields like consulting, with long and unpredictable hours, demand a subordination of personal life to the job.

WHAT DO YOU WANT?

Are you willing to have your social life take a back seat to your career? Is the job more important than outside relationships? What gives you more satisfaction—work or leisure?

If you know the answers to these questions, you are in a good position to make the right move. Many people don't know how much hard work and struggle is involved in becoming truly successful. The people I interview for my books and articles on success are truly dedicated to what they are doing. That does not mean they are workaholics. That is, they are not working just for the sake of working. They are not trying to burn off excess energy, writing 100-page reports when a memo will do or working till midnight on a project that really only calls for an eight-hour day. Truly successful people work hard in order to become successful.

If you are offered a job that seems to be on the road to the top, realize that the amount of involvement in the job will be substantial. You may have to travel for weeks at a time. You may have to work weekends. Before you take the job, try to assess your own values regarding the balance between your career and your personal life. Which is more important?

PIN THEM DOWN TO A SCHEDULE

Making the right move means not being surprised after you take the job that you are expected to work every third Saturday. You must ask point-blank how much time is involved in performing the job. Most companies are fairly up front about the time involved. But I have heard enough war stories to know that people are often forced to quit a new position and start the whole painful job search all over again because they misunderstood or were misinformed about the amount of time their jobs actually took to perform.

There is a whole array of questions that you can ask. How many days per week do you have to work? How often will you have to work weekends (and will you be compensated for the extra time)? Has the staff ever worked around the clock when the work load became heavy? And does this type of thing occur often?

If you are lucky, one of your interviews will take place between twelve and two, thus affording you the opportunity to observe how many people are eating lunch at their desks. Lunch hour ceases to be part of your free time when it consists of gulping down a sandwich and soda while talking on the phone with a client.

You should also ask about "comp time." This term refers to the hours that the company gives you back to compensate for the extra time you have spent completing a project or traveling on weekends. But you should try to become acquainted with someone already working at the company if you want to verify what the interviewers tell you about the company's generous comp time policy. One respondent was told that she would be compensated with extra days off for any hours she worked over the forty-hour week. Her first surprise was how often she was expected to work overtime and weekends. The other surprise was the fact that although comp time was nominally offered, the workload never eased sufficiently for her ever to take all of the time back. You can discover the company's practices in this regard from friends working on the inside or through professional affiliations.

Some companies have a rule that comp time must be taken within two weeks of the original extra hours or be lost forever. This rule can leave you perpetually in the position of working overtime for nothing. The interviewers should be able to tell you how long you have to take advantage of the comp time.

Of course, many jobs at certain higher levels never carry a comp-time provision. The lawyers and bankers mentioned earlier receive compensation in pay and status, not in time. But if the time requirements of your job are explicitly stated and delimited, make sure you know how often these limits are violated and what you will get in return for your extra time and work.

The Commute

The commute between home and work can have a big impact on your life. People who live in areas such as New York are accustomed to the drudgery of hour-plus subway or bus rides. And those living in Los Angeles know what it is like to spend an hour and a half on the freeway in order to get to work. But if you are like most Americans, your idea of a normal commute is around twenty minutes door-to-door.

You should be aware of the time involved in getting to a job. What kind of transportation is available, how are the roads during rush hour, and is there ample parking available if you must use your car? You may already know the answer to most of the commuting questions. But if taking this job requires a relocation, you must learn anew the subtleties of getting to work.

Companies like AT&T provide van services to move

their people from home to work around New Jersey. Some companies coordinate carpools for their employees.

Don't underestimate the role of the commute on your personal, social, and family life. You may be facing three hours or more of travel daily, time you now allocate to house chores, backdoor barbecues, or interaction with your family. These may be hours you are just not willing to give up, regardless of pay, position, or perks offered by a prospective employer.

The point that emerges is that your job choice should involve considerations about various aspects of your life. You must consider your stage of life, how much the job means to you relative to your personal life, and whether you can even take the job in light of your own personal circumstances.

Two things are clear in regard to your future in the world of work. First, companies are becoming increasingly committed to helping employees in various aspects of their personal lives. They are involved in caring for the employees' children, helping them relocate successfully, and solving their personal problems. But second, the amount of time that jobs take in terms of hours and days per week seems to be increasing, as is the number of family members involved in the world of work. The two-earner family is now the norm.

In short, companies in the future will probably expect you to become more committed to your work, and at the same time they will probably be making it easier for you to devote more time to the job.

Only when you are certain that a prospective employer is willing to make your personal life easier—if only to make you more productive at work—can you be certain that joining a company is the right move.

CHAPTER 8

◆◆◆◆◆◆◆◆◆◆◆◆◆◆◆◆◆◆◆◆◆◆◆◆◆◆◆

A Satisfying Job

Nothing can make a person more certain that he or she made the wrong career choice than finding out that a "dream" job is dull, uninteresting, and generally unsatisfying. Why is it that sometimes jobs that have the most promise, best pay, and great perks later turn out to be totally boring? Often the problem stems from the fact that individuals don't know what they really need in a job. You have to know what turns you on, what holds your interest, and what stimulates you in order to avoid finding yourself in the occupational doldrums.

There exist vast bodies of research on the components of job satisfaction. While these studies acknowledge the importance of pay and perks, they indicate that there is something much more crucial to job satisfaction: the intrinsic nature of the job itself.

In this chapter we will try to discover what job qualities most turn you on. Only by finding a satisfying job

can you be assured that you are making the right
move.

ENVISIONING SATISFACTION

What is it that you like to do? You would be surprised
how many people have a hard time getting a handle on
this question. They may respond by describing their
boss or telling you their salary, but rarely do they refer
to the quality of the job itself.

For you to know what a job is really like you cannot
rely on its title alone. You must examine the description and the context within which you will perform the
job. And you must be in touch with your own needs
and values to know whether you will find the job experience truly agreeable. In other words, you must learn
to "envision satisfaction"—acquire an image of those
aspects of a job that are right for you.

*Without that image, you are approaching your job
search haphazardly, and will never know why a particular job is making you unhappy. Once you have constructed that "satisfaction profile," you are well on your
way to making a good job choice.*

As we go through the job traits in the next section,
evaluate your current job in terms of the "perfectly
satisfying job" you are beginning to envision. If you
are unhappy with your current job, is it because you
have too little variety, authority, or status? What is it
you really want from a job?

What Job Traits Make You Happy?

The following section requires you to perform a little
self-examination to get a clear concept of the traits that

will make you happy on your job. Of course, there are dozens of job traits that can be factored into the satisfaction equation. But the following are the ones you will probably have to consider if you want to make the right move.

A JOB WITH SOME IMPACT

Do you think it is important that your job be one that has impact within the company, the industry, and the world in general? Some people will take a position that pays poorly and has terrible hours but grants them a great amount of influence and power. Many political jobs pay poorly relative to the overall influence exerted by the incumbents. A Supreme Court justice, for instance, may make only $70,000 but participate in decisions affecting the lives of millions. Similarly, a teacher may suffer from low pay and status but leave an indelible imprint on the minds of thousands of students.

How important is it to you that your job have significant impact on the rest of the organization, on the final product, on the work process? Truth to tell, many people would rather have the luxury of not being saddled with a "significant job." They are more comfortable holding a position that, while "interesting," will not in and of itself impact on the rest of the organization to any great degree.

Many people choose research or analysis jobs over line or production jobs because they don't want every decision they make to reverberate throughout the organization. Only you can decide whether your job must have impact to make it satisfying.

One of my respondents was hired as an executive vice president for a large Fortune 100 firm. The position was perfect: He was in line to succeed the president at some point, comfortable with the corporate culture and the other managers, familiar with the business and the product, and extraordinarily well paid. But within three weeks he resigned.

The reason for his quick exit was quite simple. At this point in his career, he wanted a satisfying job, which for him was a position with impact. He had certain ideas about the direction of the company, the new products it should be developing, and its marketing strategy. Unfortunately, the current president was not about to delegate these jobs to the new senior manager. Although the VP had one-half of the company reporting to him, he did not have the real influence within the company that he had expected when he came on board. The president did not agree with his proposed changes and had no intention of letting the new person make the decisions. This one drawback was enough to make the job unsatisfying and hence the wrong move.

IS VARIETY THE SPICE OF YOUR LIFE?

When you think of your perfect job, is it one in which you do the same task or tasks over and over again or does it involve a wide variety of functions and activities? Some people choose market research as a profession because it lets them work on several projects simultaneously, each at a different stage of completion. Others fail miserably in such positions because they find the variety of tasks confusing and downright intimidating.

For years factory owners and manufacturers, in conjunction with social scientists, have tried to establish ways to make assembly-line work more interesting. They have combined tasks, played with the job design, all in a frantic attempt to add variety to what is essentially a routine job. If you take a job as a manager or executive, your problem may be the opposite: You will find yourself immersed in a multitude of different activities, many of which make conflicting demands on your time and concentration. And as you move up the corporate ladder, the variety of your tasks will increase.

You must decide for yourself whether "variety is the spice of life." If you need an orderly day and week, if you are overwhelmed by too much sensory stimulation, then you should avoid a multifaceted job. You can easily find out what you will have to do on the job by asking the interviewers what a typical day in your work life will be.

A simple indication of the variety of tasks may be whether the training for the job involves rotating you throughout the organization in different positions. The company is telling you that you will have to become knowledgeable about the multitude of corporate operations and functions. They are grooming you as a "renaissance" manager who can oversee any number of different projects. Forget about developing a single function or expertise. You are on your way to becoming a general manager for whom variety will be a way of life.

Many would relish the variable nature of such a position. If you are not such a person, there are any number of positions that don't require you constantly to expand your knowledge base and develop a repertoire of new skills.

ARE YOU A STATUS SEEKER?

It seems as if everyone today lusts after the prestigious title, the big office, and the honor and the glory of a high-powered job. Status and prestige can derive from any number of sources. A high position in the firm, like senior manager, administrator, supervisor, or department head, can immediately bestow honor on the incumbent. Or recognition of the name and reputation for success of the firm itself can enhance the status of its employees, regardless of their position within the company. And the field in which you are located may also bestow honor upon you. Certain glamorous fields, like radio, television, and the movies, carry their own intrinsic status. Add to the list of status-granters certain professional occupations like doctor, corporate lawyer, investment banker, and college professor.

But you would be surprised how many people get their intrinsic job satisfaction from nonstatus factors like the good fit between their job and life-style or the chance to produce a good product. Public school teachers have suffered the injustice of low public esteem for years, as have nurses and secretaries. In some organizations one department may have lower status than others. Witness the relative unimportance accorded human resources departments in many companies. People in these fields are motivated by factors other than status.

You must ask yourself just how important it is that there be status attached to your job, your company, and your field.

AUTHORITY

This is related to but essentially different from impact. Here we are not just talking about the effect your job will have on the rest of the organization and its end product. We are really dealing here with the number of people, resources, and even budget that you control.

If you need a job with authority, don't choose consulting as a career. Even though you may find the work intrinsically satisfying, and though your firm may be laden with status and prestige, your role will be strictly that of an advisor. Consultants can recommend change but can't mandate it.

Authority means having the formal ability to tell others what to do and enjoying the support of the organization in your efforts. Some people do not consider a job fulfilling unless they have the power to make decisions and order others to implement them. If you are one of these people, know for certain just what degree of power you will have to make decisions. You will be miserable if you cannot originate and implement your own ideas. Obviously, you must find out whether you will have a staff, a good budget, the power to spend, and a defined sphere of influence.

You should also try to discover how much direction you must take. Often people who need authority to make their jobs satisfying correspondingly don't want to be overmanaged. Not that they resent having mandates, projects, and requirements that originate from above. They are like one of my respondents, who—before she took a position—told her prospective manager that she would prefer not to be managed closely. She became convinced that this position represented the right move only when he assured her that while he would initiate some of her projects, she could oversee the way she and her staff carried them out.

THE CHANCE TO USE YOUR SKILLS

I often hear complaints from workers who feel that they were hired under false pretenses. It is not that the company reneged on the agreed-on pay and title or that the company misled them about the benefits and perks. Their discontent is based on the fact that the company won't use their skills to the fullest. One recent Ph.D., who just finished a dissertation utilizing state-of-the-art statistical methods, took a position in evaluation research. He fully expected that his job would require him to make full use of his knowledge and skills. Instead, the position requires only a rudimentary statistical ability. To say the least, this person is bored and disappointed.

Some of my respondents found themselves in a slightly different quandary. They discovered that the company hired them to develop skills in an area they have little interest in and that is completely alien to their long-term goals. Another respondent was hired by a large research company supposedly as a statistical analyst. Only later did she discover that the company really wanted her to become an administrator, a role she could perform adequately but basically abhorred. Past supervisory experience had convinced her that not only was administration filled with headaches but it would take up so much time that she would eventually drift out of statistical analysis forever. Because of the company's long-term plans for her, she found herself heading toward an unsatisfying job. Obviously, taking this position was the wrong move.

How do you avoid landing in a job that, because it misuses your skills or directs you away from your skill area, becomes essentially unsatisfying? I think you should start by assessing what skills you most enjoy using. Are they leadership and coaching skills or are they skills in detail work? Once you know what skills you want to use and develop, find out from the interviewers exactly what you will do on the job. Be as candid as possible about what you expect to be doing. Look at the job description, and use it as a basis of your preemployment discussions with the company.

The fact that you are asking pointed questions about the job itself can only bolster the good impression that you have already made on the company. After all, while other job hunters appear to be only interested in pay and perks, you are really concerned about the job you will be performing.

WORKING WITH PEOPLE

Some people need positions that bring them into constant interaction with others, be they fellow employees, clients, or the public. Others find more satisfaction from just doing their jobs, perhaps not in total isolation but certainly "far from the madding crowd."

I interviewed several managers and others who, when asked to name the most gratifying aspect of their jobs, replied "working with people." This is not surprising, in light of the fact that studies have found that social interaction consistently ranks with money and power as a basic human need.

How much contact do you need? Must there be constant interaction on the job for you to consider it satisfying? I've known several people who work in such professions as public relations, fund-raising, and senior management partially because these occupations provide them the opportunity for people-contact. In that sense these people share common job satisfaction needs with actors, bank tellers, and salespeople. If human contact is a basic component of job satisfaction for you, find out from the interviewers how much time you must spend in your office alone, doing research, writing reports, or working at your desktop PC.

DO YOU NEED TANGIBLE RESULTS?

Some people need to see the product of their sweat and toil, maybe not at the end of the day, week, or month but at some point in the near future. They have to know what the results of all their work are. These people need a bottom line. For many, this is what makes a job intrinsically satisfying.

There are some positions that have no such measurable results. One personnel director says she gets satisfaction from working with others in the organization, explaining to them how to supervise and manage. As she puts its, she finds it satisfying "putting light bulbs in people's heads and seeing the bulbs go on" and helping managers move from a narrow point of view to a global one. Yet it is very hard to measure the fruits of such labor. Increases and decreases in turnover and absenteeism notwithstanding, many of her projects, like improving organizational effectiveness, have goals that are not easily measured.

There is currently a controversy about the proper way to measure management productivity, stemming in good part from the fact that no one can agree on what a manager is supposed to do. Is he or she supposed to churn out reports, run a plant, coach subordinates, and process information? Managers do a little of all of these things. But very often a bottom-line "profit" figure can't be placed on the value of their efforts. Many blame this conundrum for the rough transition into management of blue-collar workers, who are accustomed to working on well-defined tasks with strict measures of success or failure.

Can you work on long-term projects that have low-definition goals? Or must you know by the end of the week whether you succeeded or failed? If you are sensitized to your needs in this area, you will be well on your way to making the right move.

THE CHALLENGING JOB

Some people feel that jobs with deadlines, difficult goals, and a high degree of pressure provide a dynamic tension that spurs their creativity and encourages their sense of innovation. Others, like some we met in Chapter 7, buckle under and fail miserably.

Are you one of those people who needs constant challenge, who needs to accomplish difficult goals and learn new skills? Many investment bankers I have interviewed thrive on the challenge of finding new investments. This type of person is bored when involved in a nonrisk, low-energy project.

Try to find out from the interviewers or from friends and professional contacts the degree to which the job involves competition, meeting deadlines, attempting the difficult project. And try to assess just how much of a challenge you want on a day-to-day basis to make your job satisfying.

THE LIST GOES ON

Of course, these are only a few of the elements that go into making a job satisfying. Volumes have been written on the subject, and there is no end to the list of what individual employees find gratifying in their work life. Some people need jobs that offer them the chance to make a deep contribution to society. People with this need become artists, writers, missionaries, social workers, and legal-aid lawyers. Others feel that the only satisfying job is one that allows them to become immersed in a wealth of detail. If you don't believe me, visit the computer center of any major university and spend some time watching the hackers poring over their "runs" and playing with data, totally engrossed in the interplay between man and byte.

A good method of assessing your job satisfaction needs is examining your current job and jobs you had before. What aspects of these jobs themselves (not the organization, pay scale, or perks) made you like or dislike them? Once you can answer this question, you are well on your way to getting a satisfying job.

Are You in the Right Field?

I once interviewed a vice president at a leading New York advertising company whose career had followed a fairly unpredictable path. When he received his MBA in accounting twenty years earlier, he was ready to begin his career in finance. But he unexpectedly received an offer from a consulting company to work on one of its teams reorganizing a client company. While on the team he was exposed to the enterpreneurial style of the project leader, an innovator whose influence changed our hero's life. After two years observing this person and the satisfaction he gained from the life of a maverick consultant, the young MBA dropped his interest in accounting and started his own advertising firm. For the next twenty years he pursued a successful enterpreneurial career, at one point creating an advertising company that became one of the largest in Asia.

In those first two years as a consultant he found out what kind of job and field satisfied his basic occupational needs. He needed to call his own shots, deal with a large variety of tasks, and meet ever-new challenges. Accounting was the wrong field for this young man.

LOCATING YOUR INTEREST

Whether you are a career neophyte or a veteran, you may have legitimate concerns not only about which job but which field you will find intrinsically satisfying. We are no longer in an era when every college graduate comes out of school knowing exactly what career he or she wants. And the ever-changing economic and social climate is throwing into a midlife career quandary those already established in a field. Now we see teachers who want to move into business and veteran managers trying to make the transition to consulting.

Are you one of these people who is thinking of entering a new field or changing career direction and who wants to know whether you will find this new career satisfying? If so, there are several methods by which you can get the information you need to make a wise choice.

◗ Information Interviews

These are different from job interviews. Here, you set up an interview with a company in the field that you have your eye on, not to land a job there but to acquire information about the field. Your goal is to discover what the field is like, what kind of people are happy there, and if your basic needs will be met. You would be surprised how many managers and human resources staff are willing to spend an hour or two describing the field and how companies in the field vary.

◗ Internships

College or graduate students should take full advantage of the summer or spring-break internships which schools offer. These represent an inexpensive way to get a feeling for the field. Some of my respondents have accepted or rejected entire fields based on their experiences during an internship.

One aspiring attorney spent a summer working in a law library in Brooklyn and used the period to interact with the criminal and corporate lawyers using the library's services. Quickly dispelled were the images he had derived from the media about the legal profession. The attorneys he observed spent most of their time looking up assorted facts in reference books and journals. His image of Perry Mason doing battle with the forces of evil quickly faded as he realized that 90 percent of the typical lawyer's activities involved tedious work performed in dreary isolation far from the limelight of the courtroom.

◗ Talk to People in the Profession

If you have friends or acquaintances who are already in your target field, ask them what it is like to work on a daily basis as a doctor, manager, sales-person. These contacts can give you invaluable insights into both the glamour and the drudgery of your prospective field.

◗ Books About the Field

There are several books that can provide insights into whether a field can help satisfy your job needs. One such book, *Jobs for English Majors and Other Smart People* by John Munschauer, is invaluable for those starting out. Peterson's publishes a good line of books on a variety of fields. Included in this series are *Finding a Job in Your Field: A Handbook for Ph.D.'s and M.A.'s; Engineering, Science and Computer Jobs;* and *Business and Management Jobs.* Your librarian is your best friend when hunting down such books.

◗ Career Counselors

The increase in the number of workers changing fields has generated a concomitant growth in the career-counseling field. There are now companies that will help you determine what type of job you really want. One of these companies, Life-Work Associates of New York, offers standardized tests, workshops, interviews, and "autobiographical exercises" that help people come up with a profile of the ideal job that will offer them maximum satisfaction. Unfortunately, such services do not come cheap. Expect to pay over $1,000 for such counseling.

Next time you consider a job, keep in mind what your needs are and what makes you satisfied with a job, and then apply these criteria to the position. This new awareness will make you more able to research a position correctly, and during your interview will help you frame more relevant questions and interpret the answers clearly.

If you understand your job satisfaction needs, it might be helpful to closely examine what makes you happy in your private life. Are you the type of person who seeks challenge and novelty when you choose vacations? Do you find yourself surrounding yourself with friends and acquaintances? Do you dread meeting deadlines? The answers to these questions will give you insight into your needs on the job.

Only when you understand who you are and what you ultimately want will you be able to make the right move.

CHAPTER 9

◆◆◆◆◆◆◆◆◆◆◆◆◆◆◆◆◆◆◆◆◆◆◆◆◆◆

A Question of Style

Have you ever worked in an organization that made you feel right at home, where you were just more comfortable than you had been at other places? Very often we don't know what it is about an organization's atmosphere that makes us feel good. But when a company's style rubs us the wrong way, we are quick to become dissatisfied.

An organization's style can go a long way in determining whether joining this company is the right move. This elusive quality—which goes under such labels as "corporate culture," "organizational climate," and "company atmosphere"—can determine your day-to-day happiness and your comfort level. And it is often the make-or-break-it aspect of a job. The glamour and prestige of the job with the best perks, the highest salary, the most prestigious name, and fanciest building will soon become meaningless if the corporate culture is not to your liking.

In this chapter we are going to look at the concept of style and how you can use it to choose a prospective employer. We will first try to get a grip on what we mean by the term "style," and the way it can affect your work experience. Then we will examine what it is that you actually want from an organization's culture. What style are you comfortable with? What are your values? We will finish by looking at some ways to read a company's culture and pick up all those hidden messages that companies transmit about themselves, their style, and their values.

Without learning to read a company's culture, you may well make a mistake in selecting your next employer.

What We Mean by "Corporate Culture"

One person called corporate culture "the way we do things around here." That is not a bad way to describe it. But the concept really refers to something more than how people behave. When we talk about culture, we are referring to the organization's style—its practices, beliefs, goals, and values.

The company's style takes a variety of forms. Does the company want you to be a team player or a rugged individualist? Is there an open communication system or is everything done behind the scenes? Is there a great emphasis on hierarchy or can you call the company vice president by his or her first name? Many people would be quite miserable in a company that expected them to defer to authority.

Does your prospective employer have rigid dress standards? Is this a company that insists that all employees be dedicated to the corporate goals? Does your prospective company encourage an intense working atmosphere or is the climate more loose and relaxed? Does it feature a democratic decision-making process in which you have a say in the running of the department, even if you are not a manager or supervisor? Is the company entrepreneurial or is everything done by the book? Is the company culture characterized by risk-taking or is the atmosphere more conservative? Is spontaneity a corporate value?

Taken as a whole, these elements of a corporate culture can indeed make you happy or miserable. In fact, you can probably recognize many aspects of style that made you either hate or love past companies. Your own past experience should tell you that a company's culture can influence whether or not your experience there will be a happy one.

Putting Your Values to the Test

You may rarely think about a company's style when choosing a job. Yet, if you only concentrate on the more obvious aspects of a job, like salary and promotion, you could end up in a company whose style conflicts with your own and whose values you do not share. This incompatability in style can quickly make you wish you had selected another job or stayed where you were in the first place.

But do you really know what kind of style makes you comfortable, what you want in a company atmosphere? The best way to begin to get a handle on your values is to look at the culture of one particular well-known company and see if this is the kind of atmosphere you would feel happy in.

There are several companies that are being heralded as the "right" type of company, the prototype of the "reinvented" company that is supposed to ensure your happiness and make your job life a pleasurable one. Tandem is one such company. The company culture contains several pronounced features that might make you either love or hate the organization. According to those who have researched the company, loyalty is a particularly dominant cultural trait. Employees hold the company in high esteem and are very gung ho about adhering to its standards and supporting its goals. In fact, the researchers attribute the success of Tandem to this intense loyalty. But could you work in an atmosphere requiring intense personal involvement and corporate loyalty?

The company possesses another trait that is not everyone's cup of tea. Tandem has no formal organizational charts and few formal rules, and meetings and memos are nonexistent. Jobs, duties, and hours are all flexible. Supposedly, the unwritten rules and shared understandings are the things that keep people off each other's toes. While this works for Tandem employees, many of us need written rules and formalized regulations to feel comfortable and work efficiently. We need sharp boundaries and organizational charts. After all, one's person's freedom is another person's chaos!

Also, Tandem's approach to authority is quite loose. The pronounced lack of hierarchy is accompanied by an open-door policy that gives everyone access to anyone, even the president. While we might all approve in principle of the democratic environment, many of us can't actually live in it. Just because it works doesn't mean it's for you.

Tandem also encourages a cultural trait that has been widely praised by observers—the strong sense of employee solidarity. It uses several rituals to develop this spirit of togetherness: Friday afternoon beer bashes that everyone attends, celebrations on national holidays, and the like. If this were a book about management, we could dwell on how these techniques for fostering cohesion certify this company as an "advanced" organization. But whether you would be comfortable as a member of a company that is more like a close-knit family is something that only you can decide.

Could you work in an atmosphere such as Tandem's on a day-in, day-out basis? Although the majority of Tandem's employees seem to love the corporate atmosphere, you may not. You must decide for yourself what you want in a corporate culture.

One thing is sure: You will not succeed in an environment where you don't feel comfortable. When you choose a job, you are selecting a set of values, a method of relating to people, a way of life.

What Do You Want?

In order to help you better understand what company style is the most comfortable for you, we are going to identify and explore some elements of a corporation's culture that can affect your work experience.

A SENSE OF PURPOSE

Do you think you could work in an environment where people don't care if the job gets done, where the employees have no interest in the product they are working on? Or is it important to you that everyone in your department or company loves what he or she is doing and shares a sense of company mission?

We tend to think that these issues are secondary considerations in our job choices. But when workers have a strong sense of purpose, when they believe in what they are doing, their productivity goes up, the product gets better, and the work goes more smoothly. And studies have shown that both absenteeism and turnover decrease when workers are more dedicated to the product and the job.

I performed some of my research for my last book, *The Mentor Connection*, at General Foods in White Plains, New York. You could sense on the elevators and in the hallways the employees' dedication to the corporation, the job, and the product. They seemed to believe that what they were producing met a real societal need. The market researchers and the product managers had a real sense of why the company was in business, and of how their activities fit into the company's goals.

Your interviews with members of various sectors of a company will give you a quick indication of their feeling about the company and its mission. You can sense from the people you speak to during your interviews how dedicated they are to the product and company.

Don't settle for idle chatter about company goals. Examine closely how interested they seem in the process of production. How much do they seem to care whether your unique talents can help them accomplish the company's goals? Do they seem enthusiastic about what they are doing? This is your organization, and the culture is something you will live with between paychecks!

♦ How Worker Dedication Can Affect Your Job

The extent to which the company is held together in a common purpose will affect how well you do your job. If the company personnel care little for the values and goals of the corporation, if they are merely passing time, if they are not equally dedicated to the company and their careers, their work will reflect this lack of concern. And if they work in a disinterested and alienated fashion, they will have little interest in doing those extra things, those special activities, that will help you perform your own job.

If you've ever been stuck with a secretary or staff member who doesn't care about his or her job, you know this is true. Such a worker will take too much time performing tasks and can slow down both your day and your career.

This is equally true in the case of managerial peers and other professionals. Just imagine the teamwork and coordination necessary to accomplish any task, whether it is in product management or marketing, finance or accounting. Your colleagues' cooperation and interest is crucial to your accomplishing your own goals. The corporate culture can go a long way in encouraging this sense of purpose.

Of course, your own set of priorities may be averse to a company that is characterized by such a level of loyalty and dedication. You may merely consider this an overconformist "gray flannel suit" type of company. And you may think the people there undimensional. But remember the warning about the undedicated peer group and the effect it can have on your career. You will be on the safe side if you consider taking a position in a company whose employees share a strong sense of dedication.

THE DEMOCRATIC STYLE OF COMMAND

Are you an independent person? Do you like to make your own decisions? The average person would like to be involved in the decision making in a company, at least on some minimal level. And many companies are trying to include more levels of workers in the decision-making process. An offshoot of the human relations approach to organizations started after World War II, the participative management technique has been gaining favor.

There are many positive things to be said for working for a company with the democratic style of command. You will be included in many of the decisions, you will have a chance to voice your opinion, and you certainly will never get the feeling that you are having policy dictated to you.

But this work style is not for everyone. For one thing, being involved in these decisions will require you to keep informed of all aspects of the job and company and attend numerous meetings. Many people do not need or want that type of involvement with the day-to-day decision making, and find it not a boon but a burden. You may feel more comfortable taking direction, not helping create departmental policy.

In addition, a participative or democratic culture

may require you to have a different relationship with your subordinates than you are accustomed to. The inability many American executives have in adapting to Japanese companies' democratic style is by now legend. The Americans are uncomfortable not being the boss in the same way they are in the traditional hierarchy.

In any event, you will want to find out if your prospective employer reflects your values on power sharing. During the interview, ask how decisions are made. Find out if the company now has or plans to institute a formal participative or consensus-based committee system. You can often discover the company's tendencies toward power sharing from the interviewers' reactions to your suggestions and plans for improvement of established procedures. Note especially their enthusiasm when you state your desire for power and to have a say in the running of the organization.

IS THE COMPANY DEDICATED TO EXCELLENCE?

Another style issue that may determine whether you are making the right move in taking a position is the level of dedication to excellence demonstrated by the company.

At Control Data Corporation, almost every facility has its own training center, equipped with PLATO computer terminals to enhance and simplify self-teaching techniques. These terminals bring to the worker's world a whole battery of courses that can help him or her become a better worker. Each manager and employee is required to spend at least forty hours a year in training.

Not only does the company demand excellence, the

workers there are only too happy to respond to this
mandate. On average, each manager exceeded his or
her minimum requirement by seven hours. Since the
company should run more smoothly with a well-
trained work force in place, your own job should be
easier to perform. But you also face more stringent
performance expectations. For instance, you will be
expected to keep yourself abreast of the latest developments in computers.

As we mentioned in Chapter 5, training forms an
important underpinning of your job performance. A
company that is willing to train you is one that wants
to see you succeed. But because you are being trained
that much more thoroughly in a corporate culture per-
meated with the excellence ethic, there are much
greater expectations in regard to your performance.

Because an "excellence" culture has a unique set of
standards, this type of company is not for everyone.

*Only you can decide whether you want to reach the
heights of performance or whether you just want to collect a check.*

Open Communication: The Key to Job Happiness?

Does it make a difference to you whether you know
exactly what is going on at all company levels? Should
ease of communication really affect your decision to
take a job with a particular company? Let's look at
how some companies handle communication among
members to see how it can affect your work experience.

This concern about communication can manifest itself in a variety of ways. For instance, some companies pride themselves on the clarity of their memos and the speed with which they communicate details of the job and the organization to the workers.

One management consulting firm I looked at has perfected the communication process. In much the same way that Tandem uses the beer bash to increase employee involvement, this company utilizies its "Friday night at the store" get-togethers to increase communication. Since many of the consultants in the company are often out on assignment for days or weeks on end, and have consequently lost touch with everyday staff events, the company ensures that communication remains high by insisting that every member of the company make an appearance at the Friday parties.

Why should you be concerned whether a prospective employer holds regular staff get-togethers such as parties and beer bashes? The answer to this question lies in the fact that an "open communications" corporate culture can make it easier to perform your new job and succeed in the company. For example, these parties often provide an informal link between you and the rest of the organization which gives you access to resources, people, and information that would otherwise be unavailable to you. Since your ability to perform this job is dependent on access to such skills and information, you should heed well whether the company has provided mechanisms, such as regular informal get-togethers, to ease the communications patterns that exist among members and between hierarchies.

Do You Need a Structured Environment?

Weichert Realtors is an expanding company that requires specially talented workers. It is generally known that they need a person who can simultaneously act independently yet avoid the maverick label.

The center of the cyclone, as it were, is the owner and founder, Jim Weichert, a forty-year-old multimillionaire. Even though the real estate company has a total staff now reaching several hundred, he participates in all the major hiring. He is considered by many to be charismatic, even evangelical, and his personality makes a strong imprint on the corporate culture. He has infused the average worker with the "excellence ethic."

While this is not a high-risk environment (this is a middleman type of company that depends on marketing rather than manufacturing to turn a profit), it certainly needs self-starters and inventive types. Even those working in the management information systems end, a typically "straight-conservative" environment, have learned that Jim Weichert values cunning, inventiveness, and the ability to change direction and assume new projects. This atmosphere can be extremely wearing on some. I asked a Weichert worker involved in the employee selection process just how they ensure that they get the type of individual who can work in an unstructured environment.

> We merely ask the person on the interview exactly how he would approach a problem. If he starts quoting chapter and verse about the "right way" of doing the job, we quickly end the interview. But

if he tells us that he looks at a problem and responds intuitively, then we know we have a potential winner.

Every employee knows that change is an essential ingredient of the management style, something rooted in the Jim Weichert approach to business. According to one worker there, the leader may think that the company should depend on multiple listings to sell houses one day, and after the marketing department establishes the requisite procedures, Weichert may tell them that the new strategy is television advertising.

This atmosphere of change could be extremely frustrating to a "by-the-rules" type of person. Could you survive in an environment that requires constant change? This particular respondent adapted only by unlearning several years of rulebook behavior ingested during an earlier stay at one of the more staid computer giants.

Such an environment of change requires employees to contribute both new ideas and hard work. Long hours and long weeks are the norm. And the closer employees get to dealing with the commander in chief on a daily basis (which tends to occur more as one moves up the corporate ladder), the more they are expected to be accustomed to change and ready to contribute.

"The people who end up working closely with Weichert are neither yes-men nor prima donnas." This person is suggesting that on the one hand the worker there has to be ready to contradict the boss but on the other be prepared to acquiesce in the changes and rules agreed on by the firm.

We spoke earlier about your willingness to be part

of the decision-making process. At this firm that value is really tested, because Mr. Weichert could very well walk up to you and ask you your opinion about the direction of the company for the next month or year. At first the average employee—accustomed to being told what to do and how to do it—is often cowed by this type of encounter.

At Weichert the unstructured environment forces the worker to participate. Since the hierarchy is amorphous, your chance really to contribute would be substantial. But there is a responsibility that accompanies such an oppoortunity. You will have to be inventive and creative in your responses to change.

You can easily detect a company's level of structure. For instance, you could merely ask during the interview how decisions are made and what you would do on a day-to-day basis. You could find out just what is expected of you and then ask how you are to accomplish such tasks.

Of course, as just indicated, places like Weichert will make your investigation easy. Since change is such an important part of the work process, they already have set questions they use during the interview that eliminate the straight-and-narrow mind from the hiring pool.

But finding out whether or not the company has a structured hierarchy is only half your assignment. Equally important is determining what you want in terms of structure and responsibility.

Do you want a company where change is a way of life? Would you feel comfortable in an unstructured environment with few rules of behavior? Only when you get in touch with your values regarding these issues will you be certain you can make the right move.

PRIVACY: THE STYLE ISSUE OF THE 1980s

We spoke earlier about your office as a perk, a way to establish your organizational status. But the physical setting will also affect the quality of your work life. Whether you are a secretary, dental hygienist, manager, or company president, the atmosphere at your company can very well be affected by the shape of your office.

Since the 1960s, there has been a concerted movement to eliminate walled offices from the corporate workplace. In the name of increased communication, a generation of designers has developed office areas characterized by open spaces and low or no walls. An open office can be anything from a desk in the middle of the floor to a semienclosed area with high partitions.

Companies are now beginning to reevaluate the push to the open office. They are discovering that their employees need status and privacy. Gradually employees begin to use plants and other creative accoutrements to subdivide this open atmosphere. They perceive what the new-age architects call "horizontal communication" as distracting chatter. Some complain that they are constantly forced to listen to coworkers' phone calls and conversations. While this physical setup leads to many interesting encounters with fellow employees throughout the day, it also interferes with productivity.

Some companies are responding to these findings by giving their managers closed offices again. But, in spite of some improvements, don't be surprised if your prospective employer offers you not your own closed office but a "work station," regardless of your position in the hierarchy.

You must evaluate your need for privacy to ascertain whether the company you are considering joining has the amount of seclusion you need to get your work done. Some people are driven to distraction by the open systems that are a feature of modern companies. Others think it's just great to be able to socialize and exchange ideas so freely and would feel claustrophobic in a private office.

Before taking a position, don't hesitate to inquire about your working space. You should even ask to see the exact place where you will do most of your work. Remember, the structure of your work environment can greatly affect your work experience.

IS THE COMPANY CONCERNED ABOUT ITS WORKERS?

Another cultural trait is the extent to which your prospective company truly cares about its people. You may get the just rewards discussed in Chapter 4, your own job may be satisfying, and the company may suit your life-style. But you may be miserable if the culture does not exhibit the family feeling that says "we are all part of the team and the company is pulling for us to do well."

According to some of its employees, Bristol-Myers uses a variety of methods to convince its workers that it needs and cares for them. It instituted what it calls service anniversary luncheons for rank-and-file clericals, line workers, and secretaries, at which the top-echelon personnel rub elbows with the "common laborers." The company has a strong human resources policy that utilizes local and divisional house organs to instill a family spirit. It also features a Quarter Century Club for twenty-five-year employees, health exams, free flu shots, eye exams, and tuition reimbursement.

Though all of these efforts can be viewed as perks, they do more than bestow on employees an extra set of benefits. They strongly suggest to the employees that they are valued, that the company really cares.

Some companies utilize company picnics and other social events to enhance the employees' feeling of importance. JWT Group, an advertising firm, took 1,000 of its employees on a rented train to Belmont Park for a day at the races. Corporate Sports Unlimited, Inc., an Atlanta firm that stages big picnics, arranged for a pilot equipped with a jet-powered backpack to buzz its October picnic.

Companies with international divisions, such as Johnson's Wax, spend millions flying entire cadres of workers to home headquarters so that they can meet other employees. All 500 members of its British division were recently whisked to the United States to socialize with the company's American employees and tour its factories. Some of the British workers even stayed as guests in the houses of the American employees. Mary Kay Cosmetics, Inc., makes a point of utilizing public spectacles to reward its best sales people. The people of Mary Kay know that their company cares about them because it goes out of its way to shower the workers with attention.

When evaluating a prospective firm, what are you to make of such extracurricular activities? What do they say about the corporate culture? Do these activities make one iota of difference when it comes to choosing a company?

You bet they should! Companies that go all out for

their employees are trying to tell you something—that they care about the quality of your worklife, that they care about you. Working for a "caring company" can help your career in subtle ways. A work force made happier by a company that cares will operate in a more productive and cooperative manner. Your job and hence your climb up the career ladder will be made easier.

That is not to say that you should avoid joining Company X because they never have a company picnic or a Christmas party. But the absence of such rites and rituals could imply a few things. For instance, it could indicate that the company just doesn't value its employees. The lack of rituals could also mean that the company is so tied to its hierarchy, work roles, and corporate stratification system that any opportunity for top executives to let their hair down is considered gravely threatening to the corporation.

Would it bother you if your company did not have that family feeling? Would you mind working for a company that is really not interested in establishing a team feeling? Many companies continue on their own merry way with little attempt at creating this sense of caring.

You must begin to examine your values very closely. If you merely want to collect a check, or if this job is a stepping-stone, or if you would be uncomfortable in an organization with a close-knit family environment anyway, then you probably have nothing to worry about if the company doesn't seem to be going the extra yard to create employee closeness.

But if you really are concerned about this issue, then you must examine the company's newsletters and find out through books, newspapers, the grapevine, and employees of the company just how much the company cares about its employees.

THE "LOOSE" VERSUS THE "TIGHT" ATMOSPHERE

As just mentioned, Bristol-Myers is an excellent company to work for. But according to some of its employees, the company culture is not for everyone. Many job hunters find the atmosphere there too staid, conservative, and tight for their taste.

The company's origins had a lot of influence on its current style. The company was established by the original Bristols and Myers, English families who left their very discernible imprint on the entire cultural framework. According to some who work at the company, in spite of its attempts at democracy and egalitarianism, there is a certain distance between top management and the rest of the company. There is an unmistakable reserve and traditional staid posture that even influences lunchroom behavior. As you would expect, the dress code is formal. People are even required to wear jackets when going to conference rooms for informal meetings.

The tight company will often base your promotions on the way you dress. For some companies it is imperative that you dress formally in order to be considered for upward movement. According to some employees at Avon Cosmetics, the creative types in their advertising department regularly (though unknowingly) sabotage their careers by not adhering to the more formal dress code required at interdepartmental meetings. Those jean-clad workers who populate Avon's advertising department can get stuck in their positions unless a sympathetic mentor helps them understand the corporation's preferred style of dress.

These people might be better off in a loose culture that doesn't value the way a person dresses so much as his or her substantive contributions. They are working in a culture that conflicts with their own particular style, and they can pay a heavy career price for their nonconformity.

We have seen what a tight company looks like. But what about the loose culture? One respondent described what it is like to work in such an environment.

He claimed that his company has what he calls a "sense of play," an atmosphere characterized by an ease of interaction between all employees. The employees can talk freely with each other, exchange personal anecdotes, and discuss things other than work. Most important, people can joke with one another. And since supervisors aren't watching their every move, people don't have to watch every word they say. No one is afraid that acting loosely will be considered unbusinesslike.

But of course, you have your own needs, and you know whether a freewheeling or a conservative company will make you happy. The main object is to discover what you want in a culture and whether the company matches that ideal.

THE ENTREPRENEURIAL STYLE

3M has an almost legendary reputation for encouraging innovation at all levels of the corporation. For example, the company allows its chemists and researchers one day a week to experiment with their own ideas for products. Any person in the company, from secretary to vice president, can suggest a product idea to management and, if the idea sounds good enough to the decision makers, can get monetary and staff support for its development. The result: 45,000 3M products spread across virtually every industry. Its rule of thumb is that one-quarter of the company's annual sales should be generated by products that did not exist five years ago.

The company is virtually engulfed in creativity and innovation. Even conversations with a janitor can turn to discussions of new products for 3M.

All theorists and pop writers, from Rosabeth Kantor to John Naisbitt, look at such companies and proclaim the advent of the age of the entrepreneur. In his books on corporate excellence, Tom Peters talks about the development of "skunk works" and little pockets of innovation that seem to be overtaking the corporate world.

But the fact that everyone is praising this latest trend does not mean that this type of environment is for you. Do you need direction? Do you need to be bailed out of situations at times? Do you like to spend countless hours brainstorming? Are you a risk-taker by nature? You must answer these questions before you can know for sure if you would be happy at a 3M.

People who go into the entrepreneurial environment are willing to take the risk. They are not as interested in job security as others might be. In addition, there is always the outside chance that they might reap the benefits of a culture where professionalism is respected, new ideas are supported, and opportunities are available to those who seek them.

You must determine whether you really are a self-

starter. What has been your history in regard to innovation and coming up with new ideas? Are you as independent as you imagine? Is this the way you live your life? If not, why do you think you would succeed in this type of environment? Think about it!

How to Read a Corporate Culture

By now you should have a better idea about the type of corporate culture you actually want. But to make sure you choose the environment you want, you must learn how to read a company's culture.

We've already loosely described some of the methods that you can use to analyze a prospective employer's culture. Now we will deal with a more systematic attempt to list the ways you can learn about a company's style before you take the job. The following hints and suggestions should help you learn how to read a corporate culture.

USE THE INTERVIEW PROCESS

Avail yourself of as many interviews as possible. In these interviews you can pick up a wealth of information about the company style. For instance, during an interview you can usually find out about the company's dedication to excellence, the rigidity of its hierarchy, and how it treats its employees.

I asked a highly placed individual in the management consulting field how a job hunter could use a job interview with her company to get hints about its culture. She responded that the interviewee would not have to be particularly astute to notice several things about the company just from the setting of the interview.

First of all, interviews take place late at night, perhaps six or seven o'clock. This should signify to the job hunter that the nine-to-five schedule is not the norm at this company.

Secondly, though they would prefer to perform the interview in a lively manner, all three people doing the interviewing generally look and act exhausted. This is the way they feel, and this is the way they act. A sharp candidate should realize that this is the way he or she will probably feel on this job by six in the evening. At this company, exhaustion is part of the job. The culture demands long hours and an intense dedication to the company, and the interviewee would have to be blind to misread this aspect of the culture.

The other aspect of the culture that comes through during the interview is that not only is the staff exhausted but they do not seem to mind their tiredness. In other words, the staff is not undergoing a forced-labor situation in which they are at the office against their will. Nor are these people working beyond their endurance. They like working late hours and are dedicated to their jobs, their careers, and their company. And working long hours is proof of this dedication.

SEE IF YOU CAN SPEND SOME TIME WITH PEOPLE ON THE JOB

Many companies have long periods of interviewing that sometimes require that you stay at the company all day. Most job hunters consider the hours between each interview "dead time." But you can use these periods to your advantage. All-day interviews afford you an opportunity to drift in and out of departments, talk to prospective colleagues, and get a feel for what it would be like to work there.

Many companies often do not know what to do with the candidate who must go through several interviews throughout the day. Sometimes you will have as many as two to four hours between a morning and an afternoon interview. Those conducting the interview feel impelled to make suggestions on how you should spend this time (for example, go to the cafeteria, take a walk, see the local area).

Instead, you should inform them that you would like to take a look around the company. Of course, they will always put limits on how far you can wander. But don't be afraid to test the limits. I find that there are always secretaries or middle managers willing to exchange banter during this dead time. Do the people you talk to seem comfortable, distant, relaxed, or tense? Use this interaction as a way to get a feel for the company style.

EXAMINE THE COMPANY'S STRUCTURE

There is another way to discover whether a company's style will mesh with your own job values. Look closely at the structure of the organization; note well its tendencies toward rigidity and hierarchy. A company with many levels could imply several problems. Communication becomes more stilted the greater the amount of levels between top and bottom. People also tend to become more conscious of rank and status.

A rigid hierarchy also gets in the way of innovation, and it frustrates the needs and wishes of the entrepreneur. In choosing a job with such a company, you would have to ask whether you could sufficiently express your entrepreneurial needs—be they in marketing, advertising, product development, or research—or whether the culture would stifle your creativity. The point here is that any company with a rigid hierarchical structure involves a whole set of roles and protocol that you should be aware of. People treat others differently in a rigidly structured company. But you can easily avoid such a culture by knowing its structure.

NOTICE WHICH OF YOUR FRIENDS ARE WORKING AT THIS ORGANIZATION

If you are fortunate enough to have several friends who work at the company you are considering joining, you have a definite advantage in learning about the company's style.

Not only can these friends tell you directly about what it is like to work for Company X, they can obviously serve you well in the capacity of informants when it comes to such issues as perks and company vacation policy. You are fortunate because you can tell what the company is like just by knowing what these friends are like!

Are there discernible patterns in the personalities of your friends? We all know people we would type as being either tight or loose, risk-prone or risk-averse, autonomous or dependent. It makes sense that if everyone we know who works at Company X is what we would think of as tight, or risk-averse, the company they work for could be equally tight and nonentrepreneurial. In general, people work only where they feel comfortable.

Note well the personalities of any of your friends

*working for a company you are considering joining.
See if there are some discernible patterns to their behavior and the way they are. Do you like the people who
work there?*

FIND OUT HOW MUCH THE COMPANY IS DOING FOR ITS PEOPLE

This goes beyond the perks and pay issue. We are
speaking here about how much the company does for
its people on the job and in their lives.

Notice how often the interviewers ask you what you
want out of the job, how interested they seem to be in
your personal growth, and your life. These questions
say a lot about the company's culture. Does the company think of its workers as just so much disposable
labor (you'd be surprised how many companies are
still in the nineteenth century on that issue) or is it
aware of the intrinsic value of each worker?

USE PROFESSIONAL ORGANIZATIONS

People in professional organizations can usually fill
you in on what it is really like to work for your prospective company. What makes these organizations
particularly valuable is that they encourage their
members to be honest and candid with each other
about companies. These organizations are part of the
professional grapevine. They also provide you with the
opportunity to see exactly what kind of person works
at a company. Remember, people are part of the culture, and if you don't like the Company X people you
meet in the professional organization, there is little
reason to think you will be comfortable with the organization's style.

GET YOUR HANDS ON THE COMPANY NEWSLETTERS

If you really want to get an insight into a company, read what it says about itself. Many people dismiss newsletters as pure company propaganda. To an extent, they are right. But you will get a sense of how the company treats its employees by the special awards, functions, and clubs mentioned in these publications. Since these frills indicate a company's commitment to the employee, you should note the contents of the newsletters.

GET INTERVIEWED IN THE WORK AREA WHERE YOU WILL SPEND MOST OF YOUR TIME

One respondent considering taking an inside telephone sales position with a major company assessed the company's work style by the physical layout of the area where she would be working. She describes it as a very open, "newsroom" atmosphere. Even the director can be seen by all the workers, because his "office" has only Plexiglas partitions.

She realized that the job would be performed in an open atmosphere. There was little privacy, with each person's desk within earshot of the next. But being interviewed in this open atmosphere suggested to her something about the culture that she correctly thought would help her in her career:

> *The up side to this is that when you're having a bad day and you're trying to sell, the person in back of you is selling his ass off and making all this money, and you're thinking, "Why am I not doing that?" You start dialing, and the selling becomes contagious.*

Try to get interviewed in the area where you will actually be working daily. You can get a feel for the company atmosphere almost immediately, and see if it jells with your needs.

SPEND A DAY WITH THE PERSON DOING YOUR PROSPECTIVE JOB

If at all possible, see if the company will let you "try out" the job before taking it. A company that really wants you to work for them will usually not balk. So if you can, try to spend some time with the person who is performing the role you will be filling in the company.

The Hard-to-read Culture

Sometimes it is not so easy to read a company's culture. Though you may know exactly what you want in terms of style and culture, companies often develop methods of camouflaging their cultures in such a way that newcomers are often misled into thinking the company is something it isn't. If you do not read a culture correctly and take a position at a company whose values and style are incongruent with yours, you may be in for a miserable time.

According to workers at AT&T Information Systems (ATT-IS), the company has a tendency to put out ambiguous signals about its culture to job applicants. The reason for this can be traced to a series of court decisions. AT&T has been forced to become competitive, with concomitant changes in corporate culture.

The ATT-IS culture is now characterized by a combination of many different employee backgrounds, experiences, and values. As a result of the mix of diverse employees within the company, two unique and distinct subcultures are emerging: the old and the new. The old culture grew up in the monopoly environment. Still a majority, the employees who came through the company during its protected phases are thought by many to be devoid of the skills and talents necessary to operate effectively in the competitive world. The new group, postdivestiture recruits, is composed of people who come from the competitive marketing and development world of such places as IBM.

The problem for the job hunter is this. Since there are two cultures operating simultaneously under one company name, you have no assurances that you will be working in an environment where you will feel comfortable. What do you, a job hunter trying to ascertain whether the culture is consistent with your values, make of such a situation? For instance, you may be an aggressive, entrepreneurial type who is told during the interviews that this company is looking for bright people like yourself who have fresh ideas and are not afraid to express them. "We are a risk-taking company now," they say during each interview, and you become convinced that this is the company for you.

You take the job and find to your consternation that each idea that you present is scrapped after it reaches a certain decision-making level in the company. You become discouraged when you realize that a hidden culture actually exists that will frustrate your every innovative inclination.

◗ Reading the Ambiguous Culture

The above example should demonstrate to you why you must look beyond the "correct presentation of self" that every company shows during the interview process. But how would you have gone about piercing the public-relations armor you encountered during the interview process?

By asking the following questions, you could have tapped a wealth of information about the real corporate culture and how it would affect your career:

1. How quickly do new ideas get implemented?
2. Exactly how do I go about presenting an idea (that is, who is the first person in the chain of command who sees my ideas)?
3. What specific new ideas, projects, and product have emerged from the division, from the department?
4. If my idea is approved, will I get permission to take the ball and run with it?

These are simple questions deserving straightforward answers. The responses to these questions could indicate to you the existence of a culture in conflict. If, during the interview, you discovered that the fourth level of approval for an idea is represented by a person who has been there for several years, you could begin to suspect that new ideas and innovative approaches face much resistance.

In addition, the press regularly reports on large companies. So you should have no trouble picking up cues about the cultural traits of such an organization.

One respondent informed me that at the time of his interviews with AT&T, he was offered a choice of two divisions he could actually join. He joined the part of the company that was more in tune with the new entrepreneurial growth culture. I was curious as to how he actually decided which of the two divisions represented the "new culture." According to this respondent, he questioned his interviewers closely regarding such issues as new products development, the amount of new people (especially marketing people) present in the division, the openness of the decision-making pattern, and so on.

This respondent made the right move because he was sensitized to the nuances of the old culture: a certain tiredness in the approach, a certain cynicism, and a definite lack of concern about the future.

A company's style is as important to your sense of happiness on the job as pay, perks, and promotions. You have certain job values, a certain way of doing things, and a certain attitude toward work. You will thrive in some atmospheres, stagnate in others.

Style and corporate culture will really determine not only your overall enjoyment of your jobs but your career success. If you enter a company and are surrounded by an atmosphere of cynicism and pessimism, the chances that you will both enjoy your job and succeed in it are much lower than if you are surrounded by creative, optimistic people who are solution, not problem, oriented.

Because culture is so important, you should not be hesitant to ask as many questions as possible during the interview process to determine what the company's style is really like.

◆◆◆◆◆◆◆◆◆◆◆◆◆◆◆◆◆◆◆◆◆◆◆◆◆◆◆◆

CHAPTER 10

The Job as a Stepping-stone

It is relatively easy deciding to take a job that clearly improves our lot. Who would find it difficult accepting a job that offers a better salary, a secure future, the promise of quick promotions, a richer corporate culture, and a more satisfying work experience?

But at some point you may be confronted with the decision whether to take what I call a "stepping-stone" job. This type of position, while not by any stretch of the imagination your dream job, can serve as a bridge to bigger and better positions in the future. It may facilitate entry into a new field or new company or allow you the chance to gain needed skills or experience so you can later qualify for your ultimate position.

Most career counselors agree that a good career plan should have room for this type of position. Unfortunately, many people have problems identifying the stepping-stone position and automatically turn it down when offered, never realizing that these positions can add clout to their résumés and bring them close to their desired goals.

Defining the Stepping-stone Job

A stepping-stone job is one that meets the following criteria. First, the stepping-stone job is predominantly a bridge to another position. It is a way of getting from point A to point B, and in that sense usually represents a career half-step. Second, unlike the standard "perfect position," the stepping-stone may include one positive feature, such as the ability to acquire skills and experience, but also possess several drawbacks. Third, this type of position is by nature temporary. You know that you will only hold the job for a set time until you qualify for Point B.

So the stepping-stone job is offering you something that will allow you to get closer to your ultimate career goal. What are these "goodies" that make a stepping-stone job a desirable choice? And under what conditions should you take the plunge and go with one of these jobs? Here are some good reasons for you to strongly consider the stepping-stone job.

THE COMPANY AS A TRAINING GROUND

Very often it is worth taking a job just for the training it provides. This is especially true if you are a new job applicant or recent college graduate. You may come out of school with an MBA or an academic background in finance, marketing, or management, but sometimes you can't get that first good job without having on-the-job experience.

There are some companies that are known for having a good in-house training program or providing a solid grounding in certain skills. They may offer little in the way of perks or salary but have an excellent one-year training program that can greatly increase your marketability. For example, the thorough grounding in marketing and packaging that many employees receive at Procter & Gamble makes them widely sought and often fiercely pursued by marketing departments of other Fortune 500 companies.

Many young job hunters who feel they should start at the top, express disdain toward the idea of working for a small or medium-size company. But these people may get better training at one of these companies. While many Fortune 500 companies consider their new recruits mere apprentices unprepared to participate in important corporate projects, small and medium-size companies often give a relative neophyte the opportunity to get involved in some very critical programs. Your big-project experience in a stepping-stone position will increase immeasurably your qualifications for a good job with a prestigious company somewhere down the career path. Hence, it is worth taking a few years to establish experience credits at a lesser firm.

These stepping-stone jobs also provide valuable experience by giving you a free or low-cost education. If you don't yet meet the formal education requirements for your "ultimate job," consider taking a position that can provide you with such needed formal education.

However, as we will see in the next chapter, some companies are growing impatient with recruits who "take the schooling and run." Make sure that you understand any payback requirements, including how long you must stay after completing your education and what your obligations are if you decide to depart the day after getting your degree. You don't need any unpleasant surprises that turn the perfect stepping-stone job into a career nightmare.

ESTABLISHING A HIGHER SALARY LEVEL

It is a fact that it is easier to increase your salary by switching jobs than by staying where you are. This is because most companies, on average, are relatively conservative when granting raises greater than 6 to 10 percent to employees below senior management. Very few people get rich on within-title raises. They obtain meaningful increases by getting promoted out of their jobs or by changing companies.

So you may find it easier to go with another company just to establish a higher salary level. The reason that such a job may be a stepping-stone is because in spite of its higher salary it could involve one or more negative components. For instance, in order to establish yourself in this higher income bracket, you may be leaving a good position in a high-status company for a low-prestige job in a smaller, less financially stable company.

Even new entrants into the labor force, who are not faced with the decision to leave a current employer, can use the stepping-stone approach to increase their salary base. I know several newly minted social science Ph.D.'s who have their eyes on one prestigious research institute. The firm starts all recently graduated Ph.D.'s at the research analyst level, and pays them all the same salary (in the mid-$20,000 range). They only

pay anyone starting in this position more if that applicant is already working somewhere else and has established a higher salary base there. In these cases, the
institute has a policy of matching the recruit's present
salary.

The mistake most of the new Ph.D.'s make is to
apply to this company straight out of school. The really
clever ones take a stepping-stone job at a less prestigious firm or with the government. These other employers, hungry to get their hands on these Ph.D.'s,
will pay considerably more than the research institute
for their services. Six months later these smart job
hunters apply to the research institute, their original
choice, and end up getting offers that match their current salary, which can be from $5,000 to $10,000 higher
than the institute would have paid them if they had
applied right out of school.

When is it worth taking a position for money only?
A few conditions may warrant doing so. First, if you
feel that at your current job you are locked into a certain salary level, and have little chance of making a
real upward move in earnings, you may want to use
a more lucrative though less desirable job to establish
a new monetary benchmark. Second, if you are leaving a good company to get the higher salary, and feel
that you will have easy entrée back into the world of
the prestigious, established companies after serving
time in the stepping-stone job, consider strongly the
temporary position. Third, you can take a stepping-
stone job to establish a new salary range as long as you
are not pricing yourself out of the market. Believe it or
not, there are laid-off executives and others who are
currently collecting unemployment checks solely because no company will match their last salary.

There is a trick that many executives use to avoid the problem of overpricing themselves for the next job. They take the extra compensation in nonsalary items like bonuses and perks. Thus, when they apply for the next job, they can negotiate on the basis of their current position's nominal salary. In that way, they have their cake and eat it too.

Remember, you are attempting here to establish a new career salary level, one that can be matched without much hesitation by the next company.

A BETTER TITLE OR POSITION

Of course, to make that new salary level permanent, it's good to have an impressive title to go with it. The following will show you what I mean.

One major communications company has an organizational chart with so many rungs that a quick climb up the hierarchy is almost impossible. Each rung has the word "associate" or "assistant" attached to it. The problem for the employee is not the salary, which usually falls somewhere between healthy and lucrative. I surprised an employee at this company, a woman in her mid-thirties, with the news that if she went looking for a job tomorrow few companies would match her $70,000 salary. It's not that she doesn't have the skill or experience to warrant such a salary. Her problem is that her employer, because of the vagaries of the organizational chart, labels her position "assistant manager."

What does this title imply to you? For many, it sounds like someone who runs the day-to-day operations at the corner fast-food restaurant. In actuality, she supervises dozens of people and administers a multimillion-dollar budget. In her case the company, because of its many layers of management, appends the word "assistant," as in "administrative assistant," to her rank. Who outside this company would pay such a high salary for a former assistant *anything*? What she needs is an equivalent-paying job with a more impressive title.

Although a job may qualify as a good stepping-stone in your career if it confers a loftier title on you, adhere to some of these rules before taking a job based mainly on its title or rank. First, be careful that you don't sacrifice too much for a better title. Many executive recruiters I speak to feel that a salary cut is rarely justified to get a better title. A lateral salary move that brings you a better title is acceptable. Second, the increase in title should not be too unrealistic. Remember, your résumé reflects your career progress. Moving from assistant supervisor to senior vice president will cause suspicion in later job interviews. Hence, make sure your new title "flows naturally" from the one before.

Lastly, if the stepping-stone company is offering you a title that represents a strategic career transition, take it. For instance, if by taking a job you will establish yourself in middle management, even a lateral move in salary would warrant taking such a position. And, certainly, the first move into senior management may justify joining a stepping-stone company that you have little interest in as a permanent home.

Remember, all stepping-stone jobs are by nature temporary. You take them because they are helping you gain something down the line. They are not an end in themselves. Use them for what you need.

GETTING EXPERIENCE

There is an old adage that you can't get hired without experience, but you can't get experience without someone first hiring you. Very often, if you want to get a quality position with a good company, you must produce a résumé that shows you have the required experience, usually indicated by the sum total of your impressive affiliations and jobs. For many job hunters, the only way to develop such a résumé is by serving time in several stepping-stone jobs.

It is a fact of life that these positions don't necessarily increase your skill level to any great degree. In point of fact, many major companies could probably hire you with the skills you possess and provide on-the-job training to hone those skills and make up for any deficiencies. Unfortunately, that is not the way the world works. Before a company hires you into a position, it may want to know that you have already performed many of the duties required for that job. What will convince them most is a résumé that demonstrates a steady progression of job experiences that lead up to the position you are applying for.

A journalist I know was probably talented enough to work on a major paper when he graduated from college as a journalism major. But the odds were slim-to-none that he would attain his ultimate career goal —to work for the *New York Times*—as a neophyte journalist just out of college. The only way he would ever hit the big time was by holding a series of stepping-stone jobs. Positions with local papers followed by reporting jobs with medium-size major papers laid the groundwork for a position with the *Times*. Several years of clips from these other papers eventually convinced the New York giant to give him a staff position.

Another respondent's ultimate career goal is selling display ads for a major publication. This field is extremely competitive, and a young person coming out of college has to plan a career strategy carefully to eventually land such a job. When the respondent first graduated from college, she was surprised that she could not find any position whatsoever in the magazine sales field. Personnel interviewers bluntly stated that her academic training in sales and marketing was virtually useless without some practical experience.

Her first sales position had nothing to do with advertising or publishing. She did selling for a computer company, followed by jobs with a variety of other organizations. Finally, she got a position selling classified advertising space for a large publishing chain, and after a year she parlayed this position into a selling job with a major magazine.

Observe that she used each position to land the next one. Each job provided her with the credibility to move up to the next position. She wasn't increasing her skill level at each company so much as accumulating companies on her résumé. The technique worked.

If you are turned down for a job because of "lack of experience," try to pin down somebody in the company on what exactly they mean by this term. What kind of companies, experiences, jobs, activities, do they want to see on your résumé to consider you worthy for the position? Then you can proceed to secure stepping-stone positions to fill in the experience gaps in your background.

THE CHANCE TO MAKE JOB CONTACTS

In the corporate world, many job hunters take positions in companies they are not totally enthusiastic about in order to get first-hand exposure to the company's prestigious clients. Consulting companies and other "service" firms often have a rich client base that you may ultimately be interested in working for.

Even if you are not interested in working for a McKinsey or an Arthur Anderson, temporary affiliation with such a company could serve as an excellent stepping-stone experience. It is not unusual for an employee of a consulting firm later to take a position with one of the company's clients. The client has a chance to see the person in action and is so impressed that the person is hired full time. Many Fortune 500 firms periodically "permanently borrow" the more proficient workers from their consulting firms.

There are other fields where this occurs. It is not unusual for advertising firms to lose their account executives to client companies whom the managers are serving. And there is a steady movement of personnel from the ratings services to the television networks.

In spite of the opportunities that such companies present, there is one major drawback. To take a job only because of the possibility of establishing contact with other employers is risky. In most stepping-stone positions, the benefits are concrete: You are moving into a better salary level, getting a better title, gaining needed experience or skills. But in our current example you can never be sure that you will have the kind of exposure to desirable client companies that you thought you would. And you are never sure when and how often this exposure will occur. In other words, it could turn out that the job isn't a stepping-stone at all.

CRACKING THE FORTUNE 500 BARRIER

Many people feel that the only "real" jobs are those in the Fortune 500 companies, the AT&Ts, the IBMs, the Exxons. You can't blame them. In general, the pay scales of the megacorporations are much higher than those in medium-size and small businesses. Very often there is high career mobility even for the moderately ambitious employee. And you cannot overlook the fact that it is prestigious to work for one of these companies.

Of course, it is not easy to crack one of these companies. They can afford to pick the cream of the crop. When recruiting on campus they will choose only those interviewees who have high grade-point averages, present themselves well, and seem to fit the company's image. Very often, mid-career job hunters find it difficult to crack the Fortune 500 company because these organizations like to recruit right out of college and grow their own, as it were. And when they do recruit from outside, they look for those workers, already affiliated with another large prestigious company. In other words, it is not easy getting a position with the Johnson & Johnsons and AT&Ts.

Many of my respondents have gotten into Fortune 500 companies by taking what must be considered stepping-stone jobs in them. One job hunter had a position in personnel with a small, staid publishing company. In order to make a move into a large prestigious corporation, she took a job that provided no increase in salary or title. All it did provide was membership in a good company. Of course, within two years she was making more than she could ever have hoped for in the publishing company, but to make the move initially she had to grit her teeth and take a lateral.

One of the ancillary benefits she discovered, and that you will receive if you do join a prestigious company, is the unsolicited job offers she gets from headhunters and research firms. Your affiliation with a Fortune 500 company is as good as gold in the eyes of the job placement firms, especially because their company clients insist that the headhunter canvass employees of these prestigious organizations before going to any others.

Because of the benefits of working for a Fortune 500 company, many people will actually take a reduction in salary or title to get their foot in the door. This might be one of the few occasions in which you can legitimately consider such a drastic move. But be sure that you will be making more within a short period of time and that the promotional possibilities warrant this type of stepping-stone career maneuver.

Although this discussion has been limited to the Fortune 500 companies, you may want to utilize a stepping-stone job to get into any company that you consider desirable.

GETTING ESTABLISHED IN A NEW FIELD

We always hear about teachers who get bored with their jobs and wish to move into another field. I was talking with a former high school teacher who, after spending several years in the educational field, wanted to make the transition to business. Though it was commendable that she had spent those years in the classroom, her work experience nonetheless put her in a weak position to make a quick move into the corporate world. Since her experience and education were all in the wrong areas, she has had problems even getting an interview with a business organization.

She knew that she needed a stepping-stone job that would help her step out of one profession and into another. A career counselor told her that if she spent some time in a sales position she would be more marketable in the business world. One of the few sales areas that she could break into with little experience was real estate. Many small agencies will let you work for them on straight commission while you study for your broker's license. All they require is that you have good interpersonal skills, which she has. She is hoping that the months she puts into this job will provide the background she needs to make a total career transition from education to business. Her ultimate goal is management.

Very often teachers will move into the corporate world by capitalizing on one of the more transferable skills—their ability to transmit knowledge. Since training is one of the expanding areas in the business world today, any teacher attempting to make the transition into the corporation can do so more easily by applying to the training and development departments. After these ex-academics have used these stepping-stone positions to establish their corporate identity, they can then move into marketing and management if they so desire.

If you are considering changing a field, your next job will most likely be a stepping-stone job. Be up front during the interview about your ultimate career goals. Your interviewers will know anyway that you are bringing little experience to the new field; but you should emphasize during the interview process that you have readily transferable skills (if not experience) that will make you a positive addition to their staff.

Making the Decision to Take the Stepping-stone Job

How do you decide to take a stepping-stone position, one that, while fulfilling one or two essential career ingredients, also possesses several drawbacks? Admittedly, the decision is not easy, especially if you are relatively satisfied with your current job.

You must first try to assess how your career will be affected if you don't take the job. Is the training, experience, or company identification that you will get from this position essential to your attaining your ultimate career goal? And will the job get you closer to accomplishing your lifetime goals than the position you currently have?

One of my respondents claims that the acid test of the worth of any purported stepping-stone job is whether you will later regret not taking it. In other words, will you in some way seriously impede your progress toward your ultimate career goal if you don't take the job? This is perhaps a stark way of looking at a career choice, but at least it forces you to confront the consequences of inaction.

Another issue involves whether some of those needs mentioned earlier could someday be met in your current company. Will you eventually get a large boost in salary? Will those skills and training experiences somehow materialize in your present situation? Since the only reason you would take a stepping-stone position would be to acquire something that would allow you eventually to achieve your ultimate career goal, answering these questions in the affirmative may make a job change at this time unnecessary.

If a job can serve as a bridge to bigger and better things, you should consider taking the position. Of course, you should never delude yourself regarding the stepping-stone job. At root it is a way of building a résumé. You should always keep in mind what is not being met by the job, what is lacking.

The other benefit of taking a stepping-stone position is that you can forget about some of the heavier company and job traits that we have focused on throughout the book. For instance, you probably don't have to be as concerned as you normally would be about the company's long-term financial health, impending scandals, and prognosis for mergers. Nor do you have to be overly concerned about the political environment and the corporate culture.

By their very nature most stepping-stone jobs imply a limited relationship between yourself and the company. You are there to acquire one or more commodities that you will trade for the next position that you really want. Of course, you will do the best job you can and produce at your highest level of achievement. It's just that you are not concerned about many of the factors that would normally enter into a job decision.

How Long Should You Stay?

If you took the job to increase your skill level or job acumen, you should stay in the position until you feel you have completed your training. The issue becomes a little cloudier in the situation where you are using the stepping-stone job to gain a higher title or establish a new salary base. In one sense, as soon as you get the new title or salary, you have accomplished your mission. But realistically, to strengthen your résumé you must hold that position and earn that salary for at least a year.

That doesn't mean you shouldn't continue looking for a better position. People in stepping-stone jobs should always maintain their links with headhunters and contacts. But don't be overanxious to leave this position. You have taken this job to gain certain "résumé points," and your career is being well served by this experience.

The ultimate indicator of when it is time to leave may be the job market itself. When headhunters and other employers begin to show some positive interest in you, you will know that your grand strategy has worked. You have moved your career ahead by taking the stepping-stone job and are beginning to be considered for the positions you had hoped you would attain through this career half-step. At this point you know that taking the stepping-stone job was the right move.

CHAPTER 11

▶▶▶▶▶▶▶▶▶▶▶▶▶▶▶▶▶▶▶▶▶▶▶▶▶▶▶▶▶▶

Putting It All Together

We've covered a lot of gound in this book, and by now you should be fairly familiar with everything that is important for you to know if you want to make the right move. But to tie this information together, you must understand and confront several aspects of the job hunt we have hinted at throughout the book but not dealt with at length.

Much of this chapter will deal not so much with the job market as with you. We will look at your values, and what you really want in a job. We will also examine some of the hidden factors that prevent us from acting in our own best interests when making a job selection. These factors can not only inhibit us in our attempt to make the right move but possibly cause us to make the wrong one.

Later we will concern ourselves with the role of mentoring in career success and how much weight we should give to the possibility of getting a mentor in our decision to take a job. We will finish with some final considerations that will complete your job evaluation process and help you to "put it all together."

What Do You Want in a Job and Company?

In the preceding chapter we discussed the stepping-stone job and the important role it can play in your career. We mentioned that if a job didn't meet all your expectations, you still might take it for the time being. Here we are going to zero in on what those expectations about your job and career really are—those specific ingredients that go into your concept of the "perfect job."

The following exercises are aimed at helping you solidify in your own mind what you want in a job and company. They should also help you focus on your career and your timetable for getting to the top.

CONSTRUCTING A PROFILE OF YOUR NEEDS

In order to assess correctly any current and future job offers, you must know exactly what you want from a position and a company. We all want a job that fits our image of the perfect position, but defining this perfect position is not as easy as it first looks. The easiest way to conceptualize your career and job needs is to methodically construct a profile of the "perfect position."

The following questions should help you get a clearer image of what you want. Use a separate piece of paper, and make your answers as detailed as necessary. Give each question sufficient thought, and let your imagination fly! While reading the book, you probably have been asking yourself many of these same questions in a more informal way. You may find it useful to refer back to the appropriate chapters to help answer some of these questions:

1. How much money do you want to make in your next position?
2. What specific position do you want in your next job?
3. Are there other fields you would want to work in?
4. What kind of corporate culture makes you feel most comfortable? (If this question seems vague, go back to Chapter 9 and reexamine all the elements that go into the definition of "corporate culture.")
5. Are you good at playing company politics?
6. Do you have the skills to do the job you want?
7. Are you willing to get more education in order to do that job?
8. Is it more important that you have status, power, and responsibility in your next job?
9. Do you resent giving long hours to a job? Do you have family and other personal responsibilities that preclude taking anything but a nine-to-five job?
10. Are you willing to relocate?
11. Can you stand pressure?
12. Is it important that you like the people you work with?
13. Does your next job have to be on the "fast track"?
14. Do you mind a commute?
15. Do you think you need a mentor on your next job?

16. How important are perks, health benefits, and other types of nonsalary rewards?

17. Are you willing to take a job that does not meet all these requirements but that is a stepping-stone to your ultimate career goal?

By now you are probably aware of the fact that making the right move is a complex process involving a multitude of little decisions. Throughout your reading of this book, you have probably been asking some hard questions about what you really want in a job. But while you have been reviewing your job in a piecemeal way until now, the above exercise makes you examine all your needs at once so that you can get a view of the big picture. And answering these questions puts you in a far better position to evaluate any current job prospects you are considering.

ORDERING YOUR PRIORITIES

So you now have neatly laid in front of you your needs in a variety of job and life categories. You will probably encounter positions that have many of these good features, but in varying degrees. One may offer a higher salary than another but not mesh so well with your personal life. An organization may offer good perks and a comfortable company atmosphere but lag behind other companies in terms of starting salary.

Because different jobs and companies have different positive features, you would be well advised to know ahead of time which of these features—for example, a high salary—has top priority in your value structure. In order to make the right move, then, you must order your priorities. The following is a list of desirable job traits. Look at all of these factors and decide which is the most important to you. Assign a "1" to the most desirable, "2" to the second most desirable, and so on.

___ A high salary
___ A position with good promotional possibilities
___ A company with a corporate culture I feel comfortable with
___ A satisfying job
___ A job that meshes well with my family/personal life-style
___ Good perks
___ A safe political environment
___ A high-growth company
___ A job I am sure I can handle

You can evaluate any current or future job prospects in terms of these priorities. You will probably encounter jobs that feature good perks and a good salary and others with a management style and culture that make you feel completely at home. By understanding your priorities, you will be able to assess more easily all job prospects (even stepping-stone jobs) and know which one represents the right move.

The Hidden Factors of the Job Search

So now you are closer to understanding what your values and priorities are. You can evaluate prospective positions, and have a very good idea of their relative worth.

But you cannot assume that all your problems are solved merely because you understand your needs and know how a job prospect corresponds to those needs. There are numerous impediments to looking for, finding, and taking a job that are rooted not in the job market but in the personality of the job hunter. These hidden factors can sabotage the job hunter in the quest for a good position: He or she may be afraid to change, be overly complacent, or prone to act in panic.

In order to really "put it all together," you must identify and hopefully overcome some of these impediments to finding the perfect job. Let's look at some of these hidden factors that can undermine even the most rationally planned job hunt.

FEAR OF CHANGE

Tate Elder, former president of the new ventures division of Allied Signal, Inc., emphasized to me that employees must be ready to accept that from now on they can expect to regularly change jobs. Gone are the days when the employee could expect to work for one company for twenty to thirty years. The modern corporate environment is changing too fast. Nowadays, if you want to move up you must be ready to move on!

Even if Elder's assessment is only partially correct, anyone who fears change, even change for the better, will stagnate in today's economic environment. This fear can prevent a person surrounded by good job opportunities from moving out of his or her current position. Many of us who don't like to accept change become very set in our ways and are often unwilling to take risks or accept what objectively seems to be a better move. Of course, people sometimes stay in their jobs because they offer certain psychic rewards or intangible gratification not attainable elsewhere in their field or somewhere higher up the salary ladder. But very often these individuals are quite simply afraid to take any serious career risk.

I have witnessed individuals who even when confronted with situations that *demand* change refuse to act. For instance, during mergers, people who know that the odds favor that they will get fired do little to prepare themselves for the inevitable. Because they can't accept the fact that they will be fired, they won't even make out a résumé. In effect, they are being controlled by their fears. The fear is so strong that to make out a résumé becomes a form of admission that things are really as bad as they secretly suspect. In taking the positive step of composing a résumé they are conceding to themselves the possibility that their jobs are on the line.

Of course, this is an extreme case of fear inhibiting the job search. But there are many change-related fears that subtly stand in the way of our making the right move. Let's look at those particular fears that may be preventing you from moving out of your current job to take what is possibly a very attractive offer.

▶ Fear of the Unknown

The greatest stumbling block to any career change is fear of the unknown. Often people grow comfortable in their jobs, regardless of how little they like the work or how mediocre their chance to move ahead there. These are the first people who, when confronted with a job offer, immediately ask such questions as, "Will the job turn out to be different than I thought?" or "Should I give up a good thing where I am?"

These questions often emerge from a fear of the unknown. This fear can make us comfortable with

less-than-perfect situations. We begin to convince ourselves that, while undesirable, our current situation is
at least predictable. People use this type of closed
thinking to avoid making changes.

♦ Fear of Reduced Job Security

You would be surprised to know that many people
whom you imagine to be doing well in their positions
actually hate their jobs and wish that they could move
on to bigger and better things. Very often a secure job
becomes a "gilded cage," a well-paying prison.

People in "protected" positions, like college professors and union workers, often begin to hate the very
thing they strived for all their lives—the completely
secure job. Many an academic would love to try industry, full-time consulting, or a political position but
is afraid to give up tenure. I have known tenured professors stuck in universities in the boondocks, immersed in terrible political climates and getting
nowhere professionally, but unable to make the psychological break because of the risk and uncertainty
involved in any career or job change.

This particular fear may be hampering you in making the right move. You see the perfect position out
there, but it doesn't offer you your current position's
built-in long-term job protection. My solution is to
begin to work actively against this fear and go with
your mind and instincts. The only way to really improve in this world is to change!

♦ Fear of Economic Loss

Your new job may involve a range of changes. It
may offer you a new type of pension plan, or it may be
more risk-oriented. The new company may be asking

you to accept one of those novel pay-for-performance plans instead of the guaranteed pay increases you have become accustomed to on your current job.

Very often people hesitate to accept positions with a new set of financial arrangements because of the fear of economic loss. One way to deal with this fear is to make sure that you know all the provisions of your agreement with the prospective company. We spoke earlier about the importance of an employment contract or a letter of agreement that spells out exactly how much you will be getting and for what. The more that you can pin the company down to specifics on salary, perks, raises, and promotions, the easier it will be for you to overcome the fear of economic loss.

▶ Fear of Reduced Job Status

You may not like your current position, and feel that you are not getting the respect and esteem that you really deserve. But at least, you reason, you know where you stand. Any new job, regardless of the title and the office, has an unproved quality about it. What will your position in the company really be? How do you know you will really have all the respect and prestige that the new higher position supposedly entails?

This concern stems from a fear of reduced job status. As we move from one role to another, it is natural that we should wonder how much status is attached to the new position. One thing you can do is subtly express your concerns at the interview. Find out how large a staff you will have, how much authority is attached to the job, how much power you will wield in the new environment, and how many decisions you will make.

◗ *Fear of Losing Your Old Gang*

This is not a minor fear. Your job provides not only a place to work but also friendships and warm, satisfying relationships. The job hunter begins to fear that leaving the old workplace means losing not only an employer but a whole network of friends.

If this fear is inhibiting you from making the right move, remember that good friendships can outlast your stay at the company. Indeed, while you will no longer experience the camaraderie that comes from working with these people, as long as you have been friendly with them outside of the workplace, they will remain your friends. Also, realize that you will be developing new friendships in the prospective company, many of which will be equally satisfying.

◗ *Fear of Success*

This particular fear is often the most subtle. There are several causes. You may feel that you don't deserve the step upward, you may feel that your success is threatening those you love and respect, or you may fear the responsibility that comes with upward mobility. Often, we are afraid that by taking a higher-level job we are establishing a set of expectations we can never hope to live up to over the long haul.

Often, the feeling that we don't deserve success is deeply rooted and can be approached through counseling. But the other fears, such as apprehension about the inability to live up to expectations, can be dealt with more directly. In the chapter "Can You Do the Job?" we outlined several factors you should weigh in order to know whether you will be able to perform the job competently. If you have honestly assessed your skills, the availability of training, and the organizational factors that help perform the job, you should know ahead of time whether you can deal with the increased responsibility of a higher-level job. If through this assessment you realize that you can do the job, your fears should be alleviated.

▶ Confronting Your Fears

How do you know if the above fears have begun to influence your career? The answer is very simple. If you find yourself constantly finding excuses for not accepting good offers, if you notice that you are always assuming that "there are just no good jobs out there," if you consistently don't follow leads, you may be influenced by one or more of the above fears. Of course, if you have reviewed the material in this section, you will probably become more sensitized to which of these hidden fears plague you. If any of these fears seem like familiar friends to you, you must confront them. Easier said than done, you proclaim! But unless you make an effort to confront directly your fears regarding change, all the information that you are now armed with regarding jobs, careers, and your values will be useless.

Understand that these fears may be subtly reinforced by the behavior and attitudes of family and friends. Your spouse may be telling you that you have a good job and you shouldn't tempt fate by moving to a new company, or reminding you that you will lose your investment in the pension fund if you change jobs.

The fears of those in your immediate social environment will only complicate and enlarge your own. That is why you should confront your anxieties about the fear of change and try to establish the conditions for changing your own life.

◆ The Best Ways to Establish the Conditions of Change

The above fears can make you feel lethargic and lazy. Many people often know they should leave their jobs. They are going nowhere in their company and the company itself is on a treadmill. But because they are handicapped by some of the above fears, they just can't seem to make the first move.

Many of the headhunters and job seekers that I interviewed for this book suggest a way to initiate the process of change: Have an updated résumé handy. There are so many people who put off looking for a job because they dread taking the first step in the job-hunting process, putting a résumé together. They feel that sitting down and spending hours listing their skills, objectives, and so on is a tedious chore. But the process is useful for several reasons.

First, it helps you break through a stubborn psychological barrier. You may be having a problem admitting that you should leave your current job. By preparing a résumé, you are finally taking the first small step in acknowledging that you must change your life.

Second, the process tends to give you more self-confidence about your abilities. After several years on a job, many of us begin to be taken for granted by our employers. Later, we begin to take ourselves for granted. You probably don't even know how talented and experienced you have become over the years. Because writing a résumé familiarizes you with the talent and skills that you have acquired while on the job, it should help give you the confidence you need to move ahead with the job change.

Third, and most important, you are creating a document that can be utilized to begin your job search. You now have the basic ammunition in the job war.

Many people feel that they don't know where to start when putting a résumé together. If this is inhibiting you on the road to making the right move, hire a résumé service. There are any number of these services that, for a reasonable fee, will sit down with you and help you organize your thoughts, review your skills, background, and qualifications, and arrange it all neatly on paper. Some of these consultants are either current or former personnel administrators or human resources professionals, so they know exactly what should go on a résumé.

This is a first step. Putting a résumé together will not completely help you overcome the fear of the unknown, alleviate your fear of new surroundings, or assuage any of the other apprehensions you may have developed over the years about moving into a new position and company. Only your acknowledgement of these fears and willingness to confront and overcome them will serve to make them less potent. But putting a résumé together sets the stage for your movement up and out.

You should also be willing to go on interviews for jobs that you may not be very enthusiastic about. These interviews help you get your feet wet. You may receive positive responses (if not out-and-out job offers) that can lessen your fears and make you feel more confident about your job options.

The reason why so many of these aforementioned fears can have a stranglehold on us is that we become oriented toward the past—what we have done, and where we have been. We become prisoners of the familiar. What you are trying to do by making up résumés and going out on several interviews is to break old habits and redirect your perspective toward your future.

THE PANIC FACTOR

Another hidden aspect of the job hunt, quite different from the fear of change but equally debilitating, is what I call the panic factor. Panic can make a job hunter act irrationally. Many take what turn out to be terrible positions in part because they hate their current jobs and feel that they have to escape from what they consider an unbearable position. But in the process, they literally go from the frying pan into the fire.

How do you know that you are approaching the job market in a state of panic? You may become infused with the unshakable feeling that your job is unbearable and feel that you have to leave it as soon as possible. Or you may suddenly have become obsessed with the notion that you are going nowhere in your position or that your company is headed for bankruptcy.

You lay the groundwork for panic when you ignore for too long all the negatives about the job and the company. Hence, the best way of avoiding the panic situation entirely is to evaluate the job you hold every few months or so. That evaluation strategy is fully laid out in Chapter 2. The questions in that chapter should be applied to all jobs. As we mentioned earlier, you change, the job changes, and your organization undergoes transitions. If you accept that fact and learn to adapt to it, you will be immune to panic.

THE COMPLACENCY SYNDROME

One of my respondents always seems to spend about two years more in a job than he actually should. When you count up all the periods he has overstayed, you can begin to see the evolution of a stunted career. The man is simply underachieving! He has no fear of change. In fact, within the context of each job, he considers himself quite an entrepreneur, quite a risk-taker.

He has a very real problem: He is under the delusion that he is doing quite well in his career, in spite of the fact that he earns far less than his contemporaries and holds a job whose status and importance within the organization are at best mediocre. What makes his situation worse is that this guy is really bright, articulate, and creative.

He is suffering from what I call the Complacency Syndrome. He is like many of us who become too comfortable with our predictable and easy jobs. We allow ourselves to think we are doing just fine and no longer seek new avenues of employment.

In its own way, complacency is more deadly than fear of change. Those hampered by fear know that they are acting against their own self-interest and would leave their position if they could only overcome these fears. But because they don't know that they are underachieving, complacent people often overlook opportunities for career growth.

If you think that this profile matches your own behavior, reread Chapter 2, because those questions are designed to stimulate you to assess whether your own situation should be changed.

BAD ADVICE

So you have no fear of change, know that you must make a job change, and are thus ready to make the right move. Does this mean that other hidden factors won't stand in your way? Unfortunately, no.

Job hunters are particularly susceptible to bad advice. They tend to hear what they want to hear about companies, jobs, and industries. If they have not researched a job situation thoroughly, they have nothing to judge much of this bad advice against. Well-meaning family members and friends, who are in sympathy with their current disillusionment with a job and their quandary in not knowing which career direction to take, offer a range of tips on salary, negotiation, and so on.

Even headhunters vary in their reliability about job information. The very best executive search firms will offer you clear, honest advice about a job offer, the benefits, salary, and promotional possibilities. But according to many job seekers, other headhunters will say just about anything to get you to take a job. You should be wary of any company that wants to put on the "big rush" just to earn a commission.

That is why you have to rely on a variety of sources in assessing your job offers. The ultimate defense against the flurry of bad advice that you will receive during any job hunt is staying on top of the field even when not actively in the job market. This book has offered numerous ways of accumulating information on the job market, companies, corporate culture, benefit plans, and the like. When you begin to acknowledge that information-gathering is part and parcel of your general career activity, regardless of whether you are currently in the job market, you will be much less susceptible to bad advice.

THE EXPERIENCE TRAP

One of the worst hidden factors that can defeat us in our search for a new job is the nagging belief that we are somehow not ready to make the next move, that we must continue to accumulate experience on the current job. In the last chapter we dealt at length with how to use jobs as a way of gaining the necessary experience to make that ultimate move. But the addendum to that lesson is that the stepping-stone concept can be taken too far. There are those who languish in poorly paying positions in undesirable companies because they feel that the "experience" they are gaining is preparing them for that ultimate big job. People who do this invariably convince themselves that they are "paying their dues" until the "big job" comes along.

While they could and should utilize these jobs to gain résumé points, they remain for two or three years when one year would have sufficed. Very often they convince themselves that the job is a "stepping-stone," when all they are doing is camouflaging their fear.

The Experience Trap leads to one of two types of unfortunate actions. Those who feel they don't have the experience to function in the really good jobs offered to them either stay in their current job or, if they do take a job, take one that lacks challenge.

At some point you must be willing to make your big move, attain the goal that you have always wanted. You should accurately assess whether you have sufficient experience for the big job. But if you find that you are constantly telling yourself that you don't have the skills to perform any job but the one you have now, you are probably falling into the experience trap.

Mentoring Revisited

Overcoming the hidden factors of the job search will help you in your career. So will acquiring a mentor. Since a mentor can help you immeasurably in your climb up the corporate ladder, you should consider taking a job in a company where you feel you have a good chance of landing a corporate sponsor.

The chances of getting your just rewards, whether they be raises, promotions, or power and responsibility, increase dramatically if you have a corporate insider overseeing your career. A mentor may also help you avoid the political cauldron. He or she can enhance your ability to do the job by providing you access to information and resources and ensuring the cooperation of peers and superiors. And as my own research indicates—if nothing else, a mentor can make your life on the job more pleasant and increase your sense of job satisfaction. In short, a mentor can have a pronounced impact on whether you succeed in an organization.

You are exposed to many people during the interview process. Here is where you can get an early indication of the possibility of landing a mentor in the prospective company. If you hit it off well with some of these higher-ups, there may be a mentoring relationship in the cards. Many of the managers I interviewed for *The Mentor Connection* claimed that they had their first contact with their future mentors sometime during the preemployment interview process.

WHAT TO LOOK FOR IN A MENTOR

How do you size up this interested senior executive in terms of his or her ability to serve as your mentor. Not all mentors can help you, regardless of their good intentions. And having a poor mentor can be worse than not having one at all.

Good mentors have several characteristics. For instance, you really want someone who is strong and in a good position in the company. Before you take the job, ask yourself the following questions about the person you think could become your mentor.

1. How powerful is the potential mentor? A strong mentor is one with a "direct line to the top," regardless of his or her position in the organizational hierarchy. Because title is not necessarily an indication of the amount of power the executive has, you must be careful in estimating the prospective mentor's organizational influence.

2. Is the mentor getting support? You definitely want as a mentor a senior executive who has good support from above. A manager who is on the fast track or has the chairman's eye is in a good position to help you. You won't go wrong taking a position at a company where your mentor is someone on the way up.

3. Is the mentor secure in his own position? The person who makes the best mentor is one who is secure in his or her own position. Most good mentors bask in their protégés' achievements. Avoid someone who will be threatened by your achievements or perceive you as a danger to his or her career. Some mentors, fearing that their subordinates will eventually outstrip them, try to stymie their development.

You may rightly ask how you determine whether a potential mentor is secure in his or her own position. One easy way is to notice during the interview process how interested the potential mentor is in your development and your ideas. Does the person seem threatened by what you have to say? Or does the person welcome your contributions to the conversation?

Many of my respondents have been lucky in this regard. They knew the person for whom they would be working before they ever came on board and hence were already aware of the person's ability to be a good mentor.

4. *Is the potential mentor a good teacher?* You want someone who can show you the ropes, who can communicate what he knows. Many powerfully placed senior executives have political pull and command organizational respect but are poor teachers. In your conversations with potential mentors, it is advisable to remain cognizant of their responsiveness to your questions and their ability to describe to you the organization, the people, and the politics.

5. *Do your views and values mesh with your potential mentor's?* If your prospective mentor has a different outlook on work, corporate policy, and career paths, you may face real problems in the relationship down the line. If you can have more than one conversation with this senior person during the interview process, try to explore his or her views on business in general and this company specifically.

6. *Does your mentor intend to stay around for awhile?* Even the best mentors occasionally leave the organization or the department. Of course, once a relationship is established, a good mentor will take a protégé along to other corporations. But if this is not

possible, you will feel abandoned. Occasionally I have come across managers and others who, after specifically taking jobs because of the power of the people they reported to, found themselves in less-than-desirable positions when the mentors left. It is important to determine what the long-term career plans of the mentor are.

Does all this mean that you should turn down a job because you can't locate a suitable mentor? No. But if I were deciding between two jobs that offered equal pay, perks, and so on, I would definitely favor the one that could provide me with a good mentor. Not everyone has a mentor, and you can have a very good career without one. But, because this senior person can do so much for your career once you are there, consider strongly the company where you will have the best chance of developing a mentor relationship.

You will be making the right move choosing a company where you will be sponsored. A mentor can quickly improve your position in all areas—can get you a higher raise, a quicker promotion, and protect you from the vagaries of organizational politics that often destroy nascent careers.

LOOKING FOR A FORMAL MENTORING PROGRAM

Your search for a mentor may be facilitated by one of the more novel developments in American and Canadian corporations, formal mentoring programs. Companies such as Merrill Lynch, AT&T, and hundreds of others have instituted programs in which new recruits and junior managers are linked with senior managers who serve as their mentors. These programs take a variety of forms. Some feature a loose relationship between the mentor and protégé, while others formally stipulate where, when, and how often participants must interact.

♦ What a Good Mentoring Program Should Offer

Some companies claim to have a "formal mentoring program" but really have a very loose conception of what this program should look like. If you are partially basing your decision to join a company on the fact that it has such a program, you should be concerned about the following.

First, make sure that you will gain real benefit from this program. Find out what the program's specific goals are. For instance, the company may envision the program as a method of transmitting information about the corporate culture, or a modality for teaching certain skills. The best programs are the ones that enable you to learn not only job skills but also the corporate culture and how to hobnob with top management.

Second, in light of that need, you should consider whether the person who will be your formal mentor comes from the ranks of senior or upper-middle management. These top managers are the best people to help you show off your skills and get contacts. Some formal mentoring programs use lower-level supervisors as coaches or tutors. While these programs have worth, they will not help your career as much as a program in which you interact with those from the higher corporate echelons.

Third, you will want some guarantee that you will be able to participate in this program. A claim that "we have a mentoring program" is not enough of an assurance that you will be one of the people selected for such a program.

Fourth, find out if the program is of sufficient length to assure that you get to know the mentor and get some benefit from this relationship. Some programs are of such short duration that they are of no use either as a teaching technique or as a way to move the protégé up the corporate ladder.

Fifth, you want to know if the program provides a formal method for you to interact with the mentor. Does it contain rules governing the mode and frequency of interaction between the senior mentor and the incoming protégé? Too many programs languish because the method of interaction is not spelled out concisely, leaving the participants confused about how they are even supposed to be mentored.

With these considerations in mind, you will be better able to evaluate whether joining a company for its formal mentoring program is the right move.

One final point: It is now believed that one of the roadblocks standing in many a minority member's path to the corporate boardroom is the inability to acquire highly placed mentors. Since having a mentor is a sine qua non of movement up the corporate ladder, some enlightened companies, like Johnson & Johnson, are beginning to utilize formal mentoring programs to hasten the career progress of blacks and women by forging a link between senior management and these minorities. If you are female or black, I would encourage you to strongly consider any prospective employer that offers you access to such a program. Of course, you must evaluate the program in terms of the criteria just discussed. But if the program seems sound, it would certainly make joining the company the right move.

Some Final Considerations

I will finish this chapter with some loose ends you should consider in your job search. These factors include some points that have been targeted by headhunters, personnel managers, and the news media "experts" as things that most job hunters overlook but that are crucial in your career.

SOME BENEFITS MAY HAVE TO BE REPAID

One consideration you must make when evaluating any compensation package is whether some of those benefits that look so attractive may have to be repaid if you quit.

For instance, according to the Employee Relocation Council, 21 percent of the 504 companies it questioned last year made employees sign agreements stipulating that if they quit too soon after they joined the company they would have to pay back the relocation benefits the company had extended to them. If you are an employee at any of these companies, they could try to recover money spent on your move or for your spouse's job hunt.

Electronic Data Services (EDS) forgives most relocation payback agreements after the employee has been with the company for a year. But the agreements that employees sign are open-ended, which means that theoretically they are liable for payback at whatever point they resign.

These agreements are an attempt by companies to prevent themselves from being exploited, and they extend into other areas. Many companies have employees sign similar agreements in regard to training provided to them. Lockheed adopted a payment assistance program for employees attending college in their spare time, but it wanted a way to prevent workers from leaving immediately after getting the degree. Hence, it made employees contractually agree to stay on at least one year after getting the degree or reimburse the company for the educational assistance.

Many companies, facing a shortage of qualified workers, help their workers get on-the-job training. But according to an economist at the American Society for Training and Development, once many workers are trained by their employer, they are pirated away by other companies. In that way, the pirating company doesn't have to pay for the worker's training. So companies like American Airlines make their trainees sign an agreement barring those who voluntarily quit within a year of the program from working for most U.S. airlines for the remainder of the one-year period. And it also makes them pay a prorated portion of the estimated $10,000 training cost. (The Allied Pilots Association claims that these agreements "smack of imprisonment.")

EDS has payback agreements covering both relocation and training. Its training agreement requires employees who complete a training program to repay the company a prorated fee plus interest and attorney's expenses if the matter is taken to court. (They don't go this far too often, but one person who lost in court ended up paying over $10,000 in payback plus legal fees.) In general, the courts are sympathetic to the employers.

What does this mean for you as a job seeker? Regardless of the attractiveness of perks, benefits, and other incentives, you must ask your prospective employer the following:

1. Are there any payback agreements that I will have to sign?
2. What are the time limits on the agreements?
3. Is such a payback agreement in effect even if the company decides to let me go?
4. At what point in the training process am I considered vested? That is, if I quit early in training, will I still be held accountable?
5. What portion of relocation expenses are considered nonreturnable?

Try to use your informal networks to find out how seriously the company takes these payback agreements. Of course, regardless of past practice, the company can always enforce any written agreement. But it is always good to know what their usual practice is in this regard.

Many companies have agreements that cover other aspects of the incentive program, such as bonuses, upfront money, and so on. Also, find out if you can rewrite the standard payback agreement, in much the same way that you can write your own employment contract. And, if necessary, ask a lawyer the extent to which a private agreement such as this can override companywide payback procedures.

DON'T BURN BRIDGES

Many people don't realize that the right move involves not only taking a new position but leaving an old one. You must know how to leave a job when the time comes to move up in your career. The reasons for this are simple: At some point you may either want to return to the old position, or you may need this employer's recommendation for future positions. You have to learn to leave a company without burning your bridges behind you.

Often people just don't know how to quit properly. Sometimes they feel guilty about leaving, as though they are leaving the company shorthanded, or are abandoning a boss. Sometimes they are just too intimidated by the whole situation and put off resigning until the very last minute. Or they resign by memo, one of the more impersonal and thoughtless methods of announcing their departure.

Experts agree that the only good way to resign is personally—candidly and openly. You must give your boss and the personnel department an explicit reason for your resignation. And the best reason, the one that is acceptable up and down the line, is that you are leaving for a better job. The better offer is the single acceptable reason for leaving.

You probably have complaints about your current job. You have evaluated your present company honestly and completely and realize you don't much like the company, your boss, the pay, or the working conditions. But don't feel compelled to tell your company that you are leaving for those reasons. What you should tell personnel, your coworkers, your boss, and anyone else, is that while you love your position here, you received an offer you cannot refuse. This rationale prevents the company from feeling that you are abandoning them. While they don't want to lose you, they realize that you are leaving for sound career reasons.

CHAPTER 12

▶▶▶▶▶▶▶▶▶▶▶▶▶▶▶▶▶▶▶▶▶▶▶▶▶▶▶▶

When Staying in Your Current Job Is the Right Move

We have been proceeding under the assumption that the right move is by definition choosing the best of all prospective offers. But sometimes you would be well advised to stay with your present employer.

There are several conditions under which you ought to stay just where you are, at least for the time being. For instance, you may have evaluated all options and realized that your current job is the best one for now. Or your company may make a counteroffer so strong that it offsets the advantages of the new position. Some job hunters turn down good offers because they expect that the company situation or the organizational structure will change in a way that makes their future in their current company brighter than it was at the beginning of the search.

Let's look more closely at some of those conditions which may make staying put the right move.

When Your Current Job Is the Best: Push-pull Revisited

In Chapter 2 you analyzed your current job pretty thoroughly. You looked at the quality of the company, the pay, the politics, and a whole array of work and organizational dimensions. You then examined the worth of prospective job offers.

If you remember, early on we said that the decision to take a job is a function of the push-pull factor: the quality of your present job as compared to the desirability of your other job opportunities. How do the perks, pay, politics, and corporate culture of each compare? And does your company look as if it's going to be more successful than the others?

After you've looked at your offers, you may decide that you are better off where you are. This is not uncommon.

When your job and company measure up so well to the other prospects on the important job dimensions, then staying put is the right move.

AVOIDING THE PREMATURE MOVE

Even if you do find a job that is better than the one you have and is situated in a more profitable company with a higher growth potential, you may still have a good reason to stay where you are. Though it may surprise you, even under these conditions a more conservative response may be warranted.

Sometimes we are tempted to take a job for which we are truly unqualified. We may be offered this job by a supervisor who fears that the company may lose the line if it isn't filled quickly. At other times a manager is just trying to build an empire and hires people arbitrarily, regardless of their qualifications and experience.

It is easy to succumb to temptation and make a premature move. We discussed earlier the pitfalls of taking a job that you really can't do. For one thing, failing at a job can affect your reputation and hence your future job prospects. It can also wreck your confidence. Sports folklore is filled with horror stories of the promising rookie who was brought up to the major leagues one year too soon, performed poorly, and was never heard from again. If he had been brought up after he had acquired the necessary experience at the minor-league level, he would have enjoyed a successful career. But his early failures undermined his faith in himself.

It is up to you to recognize whether a job offer represents a premature move. If you are in sales and have little experience supervising others, you may not be ready for a national sales manager spot. With a few more years of the current experience under your belt, you would be ready for that job. And if your current job is providing that needed skill and experience, then staying put is the right move.

But even while turning down this offer, you have the consolation of knowing that you have made a good impression on your prospective employer. The smart job hunter will build on that initial impression by continuing to touch base periodically with key people in the company. Keep the lines of communication open. If they were interested once, you have every reason to think they will make another offer in the future.

THE COUNTEROFFER

Of course, there is a good chance that you will be offered a position that is both better than your current job and for which you are eminently qualified. However, this does not automatically mean that you should leave your present employer.

Don't be surprised if, when you try to resign, your employer comes back to you with a counteroffer. You should approach this counteroffer with an open mind. Even if your company does not immediately try to woo you, let them know that you are open to negotiation and available for continued employment.

Of course, right now you may think that they would never make a counteroffer. After all, it was their lack of interest that drove you to seek another job in the first place! But don't be surprised when your current employer, who you thought was completely overlooking you for promotion, comes back with an offer of a better title and salary. It may not be the offer you wanted, and it may not compare very favorably with the new company's proposed package, but the fact that your current company makes it at all should signal to you just what a marketable person you have become.

Be realistic about your employer's ability to improve your situation. The company can promote you, offer you a better salary, assign you a better office, and sweeten the benefits pot. It can even give you a more satisfying job, but it cannot change company style and corporate culture. It might not supply you with a mentor. It can get you better training, but can't create a training program for you where one doesn't exist.

Tell your company what the new firm is offering. Your candidness up front can prevent you and your current boss from wasting time spinning wheels. Your company may realize immediately that they cannot meet the new offer, in which case your boss will wish you well and leave the bargaining table. Don't be afraid that by rejecting the counteroffer you have wounded the boss's ego. From that perspective, one of the reasons you got this good outside offer in the first place is because you were so well trained and groomed into the type of employee other companies covet. If it was up to the boss you would probably have received an offer you couldn't refuse. It is the company's fault that you aren't getting your just rewards there.

The one thing you shouldn't do is turn down a good opportunity elsewhere because you think your employer will eventually come through with the promotion you deserve. You want to give your employer the chance to match a good offer. But if there is no tangible counteroffer, it is time to move on. This is their way of telling you that they are either unable or unwilling to change or improve those conditions you consider deleterious to your personal and career growth.

But if they come up with a counteroffer that exceeds what you would receive in the new company, and if you are satisfied with the other conditions of the organization itself, then staying put is the right move.

THE CHANCE THAT CONDITIONS MAY CHANGE ON THEIR OWN

Another reason to stay put is that you now perceive that some of the factors that made you want to depart in the first place are about to improve. One area where this may be true is the company's financial picture. You may now have evidence that the company is more aggressive than you originally thought or that the profit picture is about to improve dramatically.

There may be some organizational changes that will enhance your possibilities for promotion over the next few years. These changes may grossly improve the worth of your job relative to the outside offers.

If retirements and attrition are imminent, you may even feel that you have a much better chance of getting a senior management position. Or perhaps you have heard that the company is about to acquire other divisions or companies and is looking to promote managers like yourself into key leadership roles.

There are numerous conditions that could change sufficiently to warrant your remaining. But be careful in trying to predict your company's future. If you have a good offer from the outside, you would have to be strongly convinced that the negatives that sent you job hunting in the first place will change sufficiently to make staying put the right move.

YOU MAY BE ABLE TO CHANGE THINGS YOURSELF

At some point in the job hunt you may have become aware of the fact that it is just as simple to change unfavorable conditions at your current job as to look for another position. If you feel that you can improve your situation or remove those unfavorable aspects, then staying put is the right move.

What are some of those aspects of your job that you could potentially change? You could walk into your boss's office and demand and get a better salary, a promotion, a fancier title. Employees do this all the time. If you are successful, there is no reason to leave your current organization.

There are aspects of a company and job that you can affect, and there are others decidedly outside anyone's sphere of influence. You can't change a company's culture, and salary structures and career ladders—especially in the larger companies—can be overwhelmingly rigid. But you may now know that you can make the best of a bad political situation or even turn that situation to your advantage. You may be able to enlarge your job and make it more satisfying. And you may have discovered certain educational benefits packages that can help you get ahead at your current company.

Becoming aware of the fact that you possess more control over a situation than you originally perceived you had is sometimes a liberating experience. But be mindful of your original dissatisfactions that encouraged you to look elsewhere. Are these the job and company aspects that you can change? If they are, then staying put is the right move. If they aren't, don't fool yourself into thinking that you should discontinue your job search or turn down a good offer.

IN ANY CASE, DON'T BE COMPLACENT

Now that you have reviewed the above material, you may have decided to stay where you are for awhile. Other offers may not compare favorably with your current position in terms of pay, perks, and promotion possibilities. You may have realized that you need more experience to get those good offers, or sense that conditions on the job will change on their own or be positively influenced by you.

Whatever has served to convince you that staying put is the right move, you should never allow yourself to become complacent. We discussed the Complacency Syndrome in the last chapter and explained how it has seduced too many employees into giving up looking for a better job. The way to avoid falling victim to this syndrome is to remain active in the job market even after you decide to stay where you are. Remember, you began looking for a new job because of your dissatisfaction with your current employment situation. You should always be exploring your options.

Even CEOs who are considered to be at the top of their industries periodically send out feelers to see if better positions are available. One way to keep yourself from becoming complacent is to survey the field continually. Look at employment columns, and ask friends about openings in their companies. Most important, don't be afraid to discuss job possibilities with headhunters. It is true that many of these executive search firms can waste your valuable time if they don't have a solid job opening. Very often, they only want to determine your availability for any openings that may come up in the future. But if the headhunter has a bona fide position on hand, it doesn't hurt to get the specifics.

Keep in mind that you can make a move at any time. Merely because you have assessed all current offers and found them lacking is no reason to stop looking.

Unless you consider yourself available, you will not seriously consider alternative offers. You must at least maintain an open mind about job change if you are going to avoid the complacency syndrome.

The Entrepreneur in You

It is an interesting fact that more and more people are striking out on their own. They are either quitting corporate positions or moving out of their professions to pursue the dream of making it on their own.

The right move for you may very well be establishing a business of your own. This is not a book on how to set up your own business or consulting firm, and I would not dare to advise you on how to secure venture capital or market your services. But it seems fitting that we should end our discussion of careers with a look at one possibility that you may not have considered. Your dissatisfaction, though currently aimed at your present employer, may apply to all organizations in general.

What may really bother you about your job, and what may haunt you no matter where you work, is the fact that no one will listen to your ideas or let you do things your way. And what's worse, you never get the credit for your ideas even when the company does adopt them. If these sentiments sound all too familiar, you may be a closet entrepreneur—one of those people who unconsciously yearns to be his or her own boss but continues to labor for someone else.

You may not even know that you have the entrepreneurial yen. While you gripe about the pay and the working conditions, your real complaint may be the fact that you don't own the place. While you openly seethe about being overlooked for promotions, you unknowingly wish that you could implement your ideas in your own corporation.

THE TELL-TALE SIGNS THAT YOU WANT TO GO OUT ON YOUR OWN

A former professor of mine spent his first forty years living under a grave misconception. When I first met him he was an assistant professor at a major university, had a powerful mentor on the faculty, and seemed destined for tenure. Because of a number of political factors, he was denied tenure but later got a position at another large university. The year before he was to come up for tenure, he took a sabbatical and, instead of spending that year seeing the world or writing articles, he decided to take a position as research director with a major public relations company. Though guaranteed tenure when he returned to academia, he never went back.

He liked his new power and position as director of research too much. Although he missed the status and easy hours of his academic job, he felt more challenge in the "real" world.

He later became president of the division. After a few years he realized that although he was moving up in the organization, he was still not satisfied. Here he was, supposedly in charge but still responding to other people's priorities and wishes. And he was bothered by the fact that he was not sharing in the profits of the company. He felt that since clients were increasingly using the company's services because of his abilities in market research and public relations, he deserved more than a salary. He was building the business but getting no return for his contribution to the growth of the company.

Eventually, he made the big move. He left the company and formed his own research and marketing corporation. He already had a client base because of the contact network and credibility he had established while president of the other company. Within a year his company was well on its way to becoming quite successful.

Back to his big misconception: He was always an innovator and probably always had the entrepreneurial spark, even when he was an academic; he just didn't realize that his career "destiny" was to run his own business. For too long, he saw himself as an employee and never understood that his dissatisfactions stemmed not from the job or the organization but from the fact that he was working for someone else.

Are you like this person? Is it possible that what you really want is to be your own boss? Here are some of the signs you should look for that indicate that you want to be an entrepreneur.

1. You don't feel your ideas can be implemented in an organization. Although many organizations allow employees to innovate and experiment, the final approval for all ideas comes from somewhere else. Unless you are the CEO, you will never have full jurisdiction over the direction of the company. If this bothers you, you should consider going solo.

2. You don't like taking orders. Being part of an organization means listening to others, regardless of how much the corporation espouses its dedication to employee autonomy. Most of us can live with authority. A few can't. These are the ones who start their own businesses.

3. You want to make all your own decisions. Do you feel that you know the best way of doing things? Take heart! Society is only too willing to let you mortgage the house and go bankrupt in your effort to prove that your way is best. Go for it!

4. *You want to take all the credit—teamwork be hanged!* The projects at work are getting completed because of your talent and expertise. But when the accolades are dispensed, you are only one of many whose contribution is acknowledged. If you continually feel overlooked and overused, running your own business may be for you.

5. *You want to take all of the profits.* Besides having to share the spotlight at your job, at best you get merit raises and promotions as a reward for jobs well done. You need more. In fact, you want it all—100 percent of the profits. This is a sure indication that you are not happy working for others.

BUT DO YOU HAVE WHAT IT TAKES?

Dissatisfaction alone does not qualify you as an entrepreneur. Researchers have been studying entrepreneurs for years now, and they have detected a common set of traits that differentiates the self-starters from the rest of us. Look over this list before you take the plunge.

1. *Entrepreneurs are ready to make sacrifices.* Not the run of the mill sacrifices that we all make on the job, like staying late or skipping lunch. These people are willing to bet their lives and their livelihoods on an idea.

2. *They have supreme confidence in themselves and their ideas.* Most of us can get up the courage to change jobs, ask for a raise, or take on a risky project. But entrepreneurs have almost a blind faith not only in

their ideas but in their ability to implement, produce, and market them. Most entrepreneurs, and I include here self-employed consultants, artists, and writers, may seem to the observer confident to the point of being obnoxious. This swaggering attitude would never be tolerated in most corporate settings. But for the entrepreneur, this is common behavior—a self-motivating device to increase the chances that the venture will succeed.

3. *High energy levels are a must.* If you want to work from nine to five or six, don't go into business for yourself. The first years are exhausting. I once knew a baking-goods executive who had a yen to start his own gourmet bake shop and eventually franchise his operation. The hands-on business required his presence six days a week for the first few years. He is now back in an executive position.

4. *The successful ones are savvy.* Having business smarts is a must. We all know of great inventors who were cheated out of their earnings or couldn't successfully market their innovative products. If you don't have a head for money and finance, you may be better off staying in the regular working world.

5. *The good ones can stand the pressure.* More new businesses go under than succeed. And the first year of the enterprise's existence is usually the time when it will go bankrupt. As often as not, it is the personality of the venture's leader that proves to be the area of greatest weakness in the organization.

You must be the type of person who can act rationally under enormous pressure. You may be a rock at your current job, but remember, in the world of the entrepreneur you are very often risking your life's savings. Your whole life may be on the line! Making solid business decisions while facing the possibility of economic disaster is a requirement of any entrepreneur.

6. *Entrepreneurs are leaders.* If you have been in the business world for awhile, you probably know whether you can motivate and lead your charges. It is an important skill in your own enterprise, where you have the final word in all decisions, you are the final arbitrator in all conflicts. While some love this amount of power over their charges, others are intimidated by it.

Those of us who can't manage others, who are not "people oriented," can get along all right in the corporate world, which can provide us a nonsupervisory position. No such luxury exists in your own business. You must know how to motivate, lead, hire, fire, coerce, cajole, bribe, and promote your people. Without this talent you are sunk.

Of course, these are only a few of the qualities you must have if you are considering setting up your own shop. Keep in mind that entrepreneurs are a rare breed. Most of us will not go off on our own but will make our mark in large and medium-size organizations that we did not start. Most of us satisfy our need for innovation and experimentation in large organizations. But until you determine whether or not you are an entrepreneur, you will never be sure that you are making the right move.

The Last Word

So our journey is over. It should be mentioned that no book, no friend, no mentor or advisor, can make decisions for you. At best, they can direct you, show you the pros and cons of your decisions, and encourage you to do whatever is required for you to become successful.

It is to be hoped that this book has provided many of the guidelines that can help you make good choices in the job market. As mentioned at the beginning of the book, your selection of a job and career is probably the most important decision that you will ever make.

One thing is certain. It is becoming increasingly difficult to have a happy personal life if all is not well in your career. That is why I broadened the discussion to include such factors as the corporate culture, office politics, and the impact of the job on your life-style. Your career is too important to be limited to such factors as pay and perks.

The people who do best in their careers have two basic characteristics. The first of these is that they all have a career game plan. They know where they want to be, and when. As I have emphasized, without that game plan, career success is a serendipitous occurrence. The second trait, equally important, is that these people are usually quite aware of what makes them happy. They know their needs and desires as well as their dislikes. By carefully analyzing themselves, by listening to their own inner voices, they know what they want and are thus able to meet those needs.

I hope that through this book you have gained not only a better understanding of the job market but of your own needs. If you have, you are well on your way to making the right move.

INDEX
▶▶▶▶▶▶▶▶▶▶▶▶▶▶▶▶▶▶▶▶▶▶▶▶▶▶▶▶

Allied Corporation, 55
Almanac of American
    Employers, 47
Aloisi, Carol, 105, 119
American Almanac of Jobs
    and Salary, 66
American Express, 151
Annual Reports, 45–46
AT&T, 87, 113
AT&T Information Systems,
    218–219
Avon Cosmetics, 209

Book of Incomes, The, 66
Bristol-Myers, 206
Business Periodicals Index, 49
Business Week, 48

Campbell Soup, 158
Career chocie, 186–190
Child care. See Daycare
    policies

Club membership, 89
Commuting, 173–174
Company car, 86
Company culture
    concerned, 206–209
    definition of, 191–193
    democratic, 198–199
    entrepreneurial, 210–212
    excellent, 199–200
    how to assess, 212–218,
        219–221
    "loose" vs. "tight," 209–210
    open, 200–201
Company culture
    private, 205–206
    purpose driven, 196–198
    structural, 202–203
Company newsletters, 217
Company politics
    immediate subordinates,
        127–131
    subordinates, 131–137

superiors, 127–131
Company success, evaluating, 41–63
Company's financial health, 13
Complacency Syndrome, The, 252, 272–273
Concerned companies, 206–207
Control Data Corporation, 199
Corporate Sports Unlimited, 207

Daycare policies
   company facilities, 157–159
   employee vouchers, 156–157
   referral services, 157–158
   salary reduction programs, 159–161
Decision to stay, factors in, 266–280
Dedication to excellence, 199–200
Democratic style, 198–199
Drug testing, 167–168
Dun and Bradstreet's Business Information Report, 46–47
Dun's Employment Opportunities Directory, 47

Elder, Tate, 45, 59
Electronic Data Services, 261
Employee Assistance Program (EAP), 167
Employee health plans, 165–166
Employee ownership, 74–75
Employment contracts, 94–95
Entrepreneurism
   on the job, 210–212
   requirements for, 277–279
   tell-tale signs of, 275–277

Everybody's Business, 47–48
Experience Trap, The, 254–255

Family life, impact of job on, 152–153, 161–164
Fast track, 26
Fears
   of economic loss, 245–246
   of losing job security, 245
   overcoming, 249–250
   of success, 247–248
   of unknown, 244–245
Federal Express, 84
Female employees, 68, 84
Financial planning (as perk), 78–81
Ford Foundation, 157

General Electric, 54
General Foods, 196
Golden parachute, 76–77
Goldman Sachs, 123

"Hard-to-read" Culture, The, 218–219
Headhunters, 68–69
Health benefits, 90–91
Hoffmann-LaRoche, 158
Holiday Corporation, 87
Housing costs, 149
Hutton, E. F., 56

IBM, 142–143, 147, 158
Inc., 74
Internships, 188
Interviewing, 59–61, 212–213, 217–218

Japanese companies, 84–85
Job pressure, 122–125
Job satisfaction, components of
   authority, 181–182
   challenge, 185

impact, 177–178
  status, 180
  tangible, 184–185
  use of skills, 182–183
  variety, 178–179
  working with people,
    183–184
Johnson and Johnson, 57, 165
JWT Group, 207

Kantor, Rosabeth, 211

Layoffs, 61–63
Leaving the job, factors in,
  10–12
  company's ability to expand,
    17–18
  company's financial health,
    13–17
  employee commitment, 21
  employee morale, 19–20
  income and perks, 31–32
  propensity to innovate,
    23–25
  relationship with boss,
    33–35
  relationship with
    management, 27–29
  relationship with peers, 37
Life priorities, 168–173,
  241–242
Life-work associates, 189
"Loose" vs. "Tight" Culture,
  209–210

Mainstream Access Job Finder
  Series, 67
Maternity and paternity leaves,
  163–164
Mary Kay Cosmetics, Inc., 207
McDonnell Douglas, 54–55
Mentor Connection, The, 196
Mentor programs, 258–261
Mentors
  choosing, 256–258

  in current job, 28
  in prospective job, 85
Moody's Industry Manuals, 45
Morgan Stanley and Co., 169
Mortgage differentials, 150
Moving costs, 150
Manschauer, John, 189

Naisbitt, John, 211
Nepotism, 139–140
New companies, 52–54
New York Times, 229
Nutriwork, 166

Office space, 87–88
100 Best Companies to Work
  for in America, The,
  67–68
Open communication,
  200–201

Panic Factor, The, 251
Payback Agreements, 263
Pay-for-performance, 71–74
Peers
  in current job, 37–38
  resentment of, 38
Perks
  in current job, 32–33
  in prospective job, 86–89
Peters, Tom, 211
Polaroid, 157
Power, 35–36
Premature moves, 267–268
Privacy, need for, 205–206
Proctor and Gamble, 84
Profit sharing, 75–76
Promotions
  in current job, 31–32
  in prospective job, 81–85
Proxy statements, 46
Push-Pull Factor, The, 10–12,
  267

Raises, 71–74
Rand McNally Almanac, 153
Relocation
    as company perk, 151–152
    and family, 152–153
    and promotion, 146
    and spouse, 147–148
Resumés, 249–251
Ruder & Finn, 139

Sabbaticals, 168
Salary
    assessing your expected,
        64–70
    counteroffers, 267–268
    negotiating for, 91–93
Saloman Brothers, 123
Senior management, 26
Severance bonus, 76–77
Signing bonus, 76
Sonyi, Walter, 53, 59
Staff
    and job performance, 119
    as status symbol, 88–89
Stepping-stone job
    and job performance,
    for experience, 229–230
    for job contacts, 231–232
    for salary level, 225–227
    to switch fields, 233–235
    for title, 227–228

as training ground, 223–225
Stress management, 166–167
Stride-Rite, 158
Success on job, factors in
    budget, 119–120
    off-site training, 111–114
    on the job training, 108–111
    power, 114–117
    resources, 120–122
    skills, 103–108
    staff, 118–119
Sun Oil, 45
Supervisor, 33–34

Takeovers, 15–16
Tandem Corporation,
    194–195
Tandy Corporation, 158
Training
    off-site, 111–114
    on-the-job, 108–111

Union Carbide, 165

Vacations, 163

Wall Street Journal, 48
Wang Laboratories, 148
Weichert Realtors, 202–204

Xerox, 166

ABOUT THE AUTHOR

♦♦♦♦♦♦♦♦♦♦♦♦♦♦♦♦♦♦♦♦♦♦♦♦♦♦♦♦

Michael Zey is president of the Zey Consulting Group of Edison, New Jersey. He is an organizational sociologist and has conducted extensive research into management processes, work behavior, and program evaluation. His last book was THE MENTOR CONNECTION. He holds a Ph.D. in sociology and is a frequent speaker at conferences and universities.

Robert Half
How to get hired?